CAMBRIDGE
UNIVERSITY PRESS

CAMBRIDGE ENGLISH
Language Assessment
Part of the University of Cambridge

OFFICIAL
CAMBRIDGE PREPARATION MATERIAL

Cambridge English

Objective
Advanced

Workbook
with answers

D1339106

Felicity O'Dell   Annie Broadhead

Fourth Edition

Cambridge University Press
www.cambridge.org/elt

Cambridge English Language Assessment
www.cambridgeenglish.org

Information on this title: www.cambridge.org/9781107632028

First published © Cambridge University Press 2002
Second edition © Cambridge University Press 2008
Third edition © Cambridge University Press 2012
Fourth edition © Cambridge University Press and UCLES 2014

First published 2002
Second edition 2008
Third edition 2012
Fourth edition 2014
5th printing 2016

Printed in Dubai by Oriental Press

A catalogue record for this publication is available from the British Library

ISBN 978-1-107-63202-8 Workbook with answers with Audio CDs
ISBN 978-1-107-68435-5 Workbook without answers with Audio CDs
ISBN 978-1-107-68145-3 Teacher's Book with Teacher's Resources CD-ROM
ISBN 978-1-107-67438-7 Student's Book without answers with CD-ROM
ISBN 978-1-107-65755-7 Student's Book with answers with CD-ROM
ISBN 978-1-107-64727-5 Class Audio CDs (2)
ISBN 978-1-107-69188-9 Student's Book Pack (Student's Book with answers with CD-ROM and Class Audios (2))
ISBN 978-1-107-63344-5 Interactive ebook: Student's Book with answers

Additional resources for this publication at www.cambridge.org/objectiveadvanced

Cover concept by Tim Elcock

Produced by Hart McLeod

Contents

Reading

1 Read about an unusual person and her passion. Choose which paragraphs (A–G) fit the gaps (1–6).

Ginni Little: volunteer bat-rescue worker

Ginni Little has formed a 'bat rescue' centre in her own home.

Judging by their loud purring, Natalie and Rupert are enjoying their evening. While Ginni Little sits propped up in bed watching TV, Natalie, a natterer's bat, and Rupert, a one-winged pipistrelle, are happily snuggled next to each other, occasionally looking up to receive a few loving words from their rescuer, Ginni, who has set up her own 'bat hospital' at home.

1

In her village, Ginni is known as 'Batwoman'. As a nature-loving five-year-old, she became fascinated by bats and their built-in radar systems, which she now knows to be their echo location. She continued to read up about the different species of bat in the UK, their diet, habitat and behaviour patterns.

2

Before she could officially become a bat carer, Ginni had to undergo some training, for example, learning to identify the species, as this can have an effect on their treatment. She also learnt how to examine a bat for injuries and make sure she understood the legislation regarding the protection of bats. After that, she was given an abandoned baby bat to nurse back to health.

3

After several months of hard work and dedication, Ginni contacted the bat group to ask a more experienced bat carer to assess whether Batty was ready to be released back into the wild. Batty was declared strong and fit enough, and her release was organised. Ginni was delighted that she had been successful with Batty, but at the same time sad to see her go.

4

They come from several sources – animal protection societies, wildlife organisations and local bat groups. Sometimes members of the public find them lying on the ground, and when this is the case, it can provide valuable information about roosting sites. Over the years, Ginni's knowledge and ability to care for these fascinating creatures has increased significantly, as has the number she cares for at any given time.

5

The survival rate of those who are fortunate enough to come under Ginni's care is impressive. Around half of them recover. The sickest patients live in small glass cages. The more robust hang from bamboo screens or behind pictures, an occasional scuffling sound being the only hint of their presence during daylight hours. At night, the flyers emerge to circle and swoop around the room, building up their strength before being released.

6

Caring for bats is an exhausting, full-time commitment. Because they are nocturnal creatures, Ginni can often be found in the early hours of the morning hand-feeding her patients with vitamins – bits of raw liver and water on the tip of a paintbrush. Others are fed live worms or the occasional insect.

A The majority of patients – there are 35 in the house at the moment – have been attacked by cats. Others have been injured by cars or poisoned by pesticides. Abandoned babies are also relatively common.

B Ginni replies that many bats which have been injured will regain their health as long as they are treated quickly. Wounds which are infected need antibiotics as soon as possible to prevent the infection from spreading.

C Since Batty's departure, Ginni has fostered hundreds of sick, injured and abandoned bats. Most of the tiny creatures which arrive at her Bat Hospital (set up in two spare bedrooms of her small home) are pipistrelles, a small and common type of bat.

D 'Bats are such social creatures. They thrive on the warmth and companionship of humans,' says Ginni. 'The comfort of the heartbeat makes an ideal nesting place. I've also had bats which loved to nestle in my hair and others that would hang on to my earrings while I went about my work.'

E Others, like Rupert and Natalie, whose wings are irreparably damaged, will spend the rest of their days as treasured pets. They spend most of their time in one of Ginni's spare bedrooms, where they can be found hopping and gliding among a range of plants she has put there for them.

F Eleven years ago, her love affair with bats became much more hands-on when she found a large family in an old building while on a camping holiday. On her return home, she contacted a local bat group to see how she could get involved in caring for sick or injured bats.

G 'That was Batty,' she says about her first patient. 'She was bald and covered in scabs. It took several months to help her get well,' she explains, telling me how she put blankets on the floor to protect Batty from her first crash landings.

Vocabulary

1 For questions 1–8, read the article below and decide which answer (A, B, C or D) best fits each gap.

In our series of articles on getting to know wildlife, we are (0) ......*turning*...... our attention to bats. Despite the fact that bats have been given protection status in many countries, many are still an endangered (1) .... Populations have (2) .... considerably in recent years because of the use of chemicals and pesticides. In addition, their natural (3) .... in many parts of the world are under (4) .... as old barns are converted, forests cut down and mines closed.

These gentle, sociable creatures are often (5) .... with hatred or suspicion. It seems that many people still have an (6) .... fear of them. Yet, it is a tragedy that the creatures remain misunderstood, and some species are (7) .... extinction. Far from being fearful creatures, they can be a seen as a benefit. One pipistrelle bat can eat 3,000 insects in a single night. In one area of Mexico, bats have even been used to (8) .... malaria.

0	**A** paying	**B** catching	**C** turning	**D** attracting
1	**A** class	**B** species	**C** group	**D** type
2	**A** disappeared	**B** descended	**C** lowered	**D** declined
3	**A** habitats	**B** locations	**C** surroundings	**D** grounds
4	**A** danger	**B** risk	**C** threat	**D** warning
5	**A** considered	**B** held	**C** regarded	**D** thought
6	**A** imaginary	**B** irrational	**C** unrelated	**D** inappropriate
7	**A** facing	**B** causing	**C** making	**D** confronting
8	**A** resist	**B** strike	**C** remove	**D** combat

Conditionals

1 Match the sentence beginnings (1–10) with the endings (a–j).

1 If you find an injured bat,
2 If the red light is flashing on the camera,
3 If you could change your career,
4 If only you'd got here earlier,
5 If I were you,
6 If the red light had been flashing on my camera,
7 Should these symptoms persist,
8 Unless we get up at 5 o'clock
9 Let's take the metro,
10 Provided you've got a map,

a I would have changed the batteries.
b change the batteries.
c otherwise we'll get stuck in traffic.
d I'd buy the bigger suitcase.
e you wouldn't have missed the start of the film.
f we'll get stuck in traffic.
g take it to an animal protection group.
h you shouldn't get lost.
i go and see your doctor.
j what would you do?

2 ◉ The *Cambridge English Corpus* shows that advanced learners often make mistakes with conditional structures. Correct these sentences written by exam candidates.

1 It would be better whether we could meet more often.

2 We would like to know if or not you will be ready on the wedding day.

3 I also would like to say that the bus was late.

4 It should be advisable to arrive earlier next time.

5 It might be even possible to borrow the books from him.

6 If it will to make you feel better, I will close the window.

3 Write conditional sentences from these prompts. More than one answer may be possible.

1 you / require / any further information / please / hesitate / contact me

2 you / turn / page ten of the report / you / find / a summary

3 it / not / for Alison / the company / in trouble now

4 Open the window / if / it / make / you / feel / cooler.

5 I / see / Jane tonight / unless / she / busy.

G → Student's Book page 162

Writing

1 Do the writing task below. Make sure you check the writing tips.

You have attended a discussion on the importance of children having the opportunity to look after an animal. You have made the notes below.

Reasons why children should look after an animal:
• education • personal • physical

Some opinions expressed during the discussion:
'Children can learn a lot, in a fun way, by taking care of a pet.' 'It teaches children how to be responsible.' 'If a child takes a dog for a walk, it's a good chance to get away from the computer and get some fresh air.'

Write an **essay** for your teacher discussing two of the reasons in your notes. You should explain **which reason is more important** and provide **reasons to support your opinion**. You may, if you wish, make use of the opinions expressed in the discussion, but you should use your own words as far as possible. Write your answer in 220–260 words.

Writing tips
• Read the task instructions very carefully. • Decide which two reasons you are going to write about. • Decide how many paragraphs you need and what to put in each one. • Write your first draft. • Check it yourself, or give it to someone else to check. • Write your final draft.

2 Living life to the full

Writing

1 The underlined parts of this email are written in inappropriate language. Rewrite them using appropriate informal language.

Delete   Reply   Reply All   Forward   Print

(0) <u>Dear Anna,</u>

It was **(1)** <u>a great pleasure</u> to meet you while I was on holiday. It was lucky that we were staying in the same guesthouse in the same village. I **(2)** <u>truly</u> hope that the weather stayed fine after I left. I remember you had another week's holiday, didn't you? Did you manage to **(3)** <u>purchase</u> those books, **(4)** <u>as was your intention</u>?

Do you remember the day we rented a car and drove into the countryside?

(5) <u>It is my opinion</u> that the further west you go, the more beautiful it is. Those small towns we saw were gorgeous.

(6) <u>Please find attached</u> some of the photos we took. I hope you like them.

Now that I **(7)** <u>have returned to my employment</u>, I am very busy and haven't got so much free time. I try to study a little English every day and do some exercises but sometimes **(8)** <u>I do not return</u> from work until late.

I **(9)** <u>would be delighted to hear from you once more</u>. It would be lovely to keep in touch, and who knows – perhaps we can get together again some other time.

I **(10)** <u>look forward to your prompt reply,</u>

Barbara.

0 *Hi Anna,*
1 ....
2 ....
3 ....
4 ....
5 ....
6 ....
7 ....
8 ....
9 ....
10 ....

Listening

1 **1 01** You hear two students discussing social-networking sites. Choose the best answer (A, B or C).

1 What is the woman's initial reaction to her grandfather's message?
   A She is surprised by the tone he has adopted.
   B She is disappointed not to speak to him in person.
   C She is delighted that he is living life to the full.

2 The man is concerned about
   A having to write formal letters in his new job.
   B getting into bad writing habits.
   C his language skills being criticised.

2 **1 02** You hear two lecturers discussing a survey about living life to the full. Choose the best answer (A, B or C).

1 The man decided to read the survey because
   A he suspected he should do more in his free time.
   B he thought it would inform his work.
   C he found the introduction fascinating.

2 Which information in the survey surprised the woman?
   A Good planners get the most out of life.
   B Risk takers get the most out of life.
   C Positive thinkers get the most out of life.

3 **1 03** You overhear two students called Peter and Lilly talking about what they want to do when they finish their degree course.

1 What do they agree would be the best thing to do?
   A continue their studies by doing a postgraduate course
   B find a job and get life experience
   C take time off to go travelling

2 What does Lilly feel strongly about?
   A the importance of achieving a proper work-life balance
   B the need to develop a sense of curiosity
   C the desirability of having clear goals

4 In the listening extracts, you heard a number of phrasal verbs. Match these phrasal verbs in bold (1–7) to their meanings (a–g).

1 **get** (a lot) **out of** something
2 **end up** doing something
3 **go on to** do something
4 **get on with** something
5 **keep up** something
6 **look up to** someone
7 let something **take over** your life

a to make progress with something
b to finally be in a particular place or situation
c to continue without stopping or changing
d to obtain something (especially a good feeling) by doing something
e to get control of something else
f to admire and respect someone
g continue, but in a different direction or with a different activity

Dependent prepositions

1 **Complete these sentences with an appropriate preposition.**

1 The organisers of the activity weekend provided us .... all the equipment we needed.
2 There's a fantastic range of courses this term, and I can't decide which one to opt ....
3 I'd like to apologise .... the delay in replying to your email.
4 His novels draw heavily .... his childhood.
5 The charity is making every effort to keep up .... the demand for food and shelter in the disaster area.
6 I can't thank you enough .... everything that you have done to help.
7 She shouldn't go back to college yet because she's still recovering .... the flu.
8 They put a lot of effort .... organising the end-of-term party.
9 After half time, the football team seemed to resign themselves .... losing and didn't put in much effort.
10 Living abroad for a couple of years really appeals .... me.
11 It's difficult to decide .... the best course of action in this situation.
12 I could tell she wasn't paying attention .... what I was saying.
13 I am replying .... your advert printed in last week's magazine.
14 The flight might be cancelled – it depends .... the weather.
15 She's decided to take part .... the radio discussion on living life to the full.

2 ⊙ **The *Cambridge English Corpus* shows that advanced learners often use the wrong prepositions. Correct the prepositions in bold in these sentences written by exam candidates.**

1 **In** that day, no one works and everyone goes to the country with his family or friends. ....
2 The majority of people who come **in** Greece for holidays come in order to party. ....
3 It would be best **of** our company if we can rectify these mistakes as soon as possible. ....
4 Finally, the water **of** the pool should be cleaned frequently, as it sometimes is dirty. ....
5 Please send us proof that you have had no car accidents **on** the last two years. ....
6 There wasn't a social programme, so I had to spend a lot of time **by** my own. ....

3 ⊙ **Advanced learners also omit prepositions. Add one preposition to each of these sentences written by exam candidates.**

1 I am writing to inform you about some problems your service.

....
....

2 There are many people who take part sports.

....

3 We stayed in the hotel five days.

....
....

4 Apart from that, we had to pay breakfast, lunch and other costs.

....
....

5 They have a good variety of food as well good service.

....

6 Therefore, I would like to ask for a refund your company.

....
....

7 I would like to draw your attention the areas which need to be improved.

....
....

8 The reason this meeting is to collect money for poor children.

....
....

G → Student's Book page 162

In the public eye

Listening

1 🔵 **1 04** You will hear a psychologist called Ron Adams talking about being in the public eye. For questions 1–8, complete the sentences with a word or short phrase.

Becoming a celebrity

Dr Ron Adams explains that people have a feeling of (1) .... when they first become famous.

Ron thinks it is advisable for famous people not to live in (2) .... because they may be more easily identified.

Ron believes that (3) .... are to blame for the unhappiness of many famous people.

Ron has seen an increase in the number of famous people hiring people known as (4) ....

Ron is worried that fame can reduce a person's (5) ....

Ron thinks that (6) .... are best able to handle press interviews.

Ron thinks that famous people should think more carefully about their (7) ....

Ron says it is difficult for the public to understand how much psychological stress famous people are subject to as a result of so much (8) ....

2 Match the two halves of these phrases.

1	overnight	a	public
2	claim	b	fame
3	fame	c	publicity
4	made	d	to fame
5	in the public	e	life
6	the rich	f	exposure
7	seek	g	status
8	private	h	interest
9	celebrity	i	and fortune
10	constant	j	and famous

3 Use the phrases from exercise 2 to complete these sentences.

1 It's not .... to reveal the name of the politician involved in the scandal.
2 The results of the election will not be .... until tomorrow.
3 His only .... was that he had starred in a film with Johnny Depp.
4 Few singers achieve .... – most have played in small clubs for years before they become well-known.
5 She made her .... as a model in the 1980s.
6 He believes that the .... in all the media has harmed his reputation as a serious actor.
7 The novelist never intended to .... and thought that her remarks about parenting would go unnoticed by the press.
8 He knew that the details of his .... would be all over the papers because a so-called friend had talked to a journalist.
9 Most readers of the magazine would be interested in articles about scientists or explorers rather than ....
10 What do you mean, she's got .... – what exactly is she famous for?

Writing

1 Do the writing task below.

> A magazine recently published some photographs showing an actor and his family on holiday. The actor has complained that the photographs were taken without permission. You decide to write a letter of complaint to the magazine's editor. In your letter, you should describe your reaction to seeing the photos, explain your views on media coverage of celebrities in general, and express your wishes for the future content of the magazine.

Write your **letter** in 220–260 words in an appropriate style.

Wishes and regrets

1 Read what some famous people say about their lives. Rewrite each sentence starting with the words given.

'People don't realise what it's like to be famous.'
1 I wish ....
....

'I wish I didn't have to do so many TV interviews.'
2 I'd prefer ....
....

'It's such a busy day.'
3 If only ....
....

'I should have studied to be a doctor.'
4 If only ....
....

'I'd like to retrain now so that I can do a different job.'
5 It's time ....
....

'Film directors don't support their actors enough.'
6 I wish ....
....

'It'll be good if my kids find a less stressful job.'
7 I hope ....
....

'I haven't enough fans in the USA.'
8 If only ....
....

'I should have moved to a smaller town last year.'
9 I wish ....
....

'I think it's better to be recognised in the street than not be known at all!'
10 I'd rather ....
....

G → Student's Book page 163

Reading and Use of English

1 For questions 1–8, read the biography and decide which answer (A, B, C or D) best fits each gap.

Antonio Banderas

Due to the success of a couple of movies, and of course his (0) __undeniable__ physical attractiveness, Antonio Banderas soon became a high-earning Hollywood film star.

Banderas was born in 1960, in Málaga, Spain, and in 1981 he (1) .... on his acting career with the Spanish national theatre in Madrid. There he was (2) .... by movie director Pedro Almodóvar, who offered him roles in films. Under Almodóvar's direction the young actor was able to (3) .... his emotions and talent fully through unconventional roles such as a mental patient and a kidnapper.

This experience (4) .... valuable for Banderas after he moved to Hollywood in 1989. There he was offered a role in *The Mambo Kings*, playing a young Cuban musician living in New York. Although he spoke almost no English, Banderas was able to learn his lines phonetically and later took intensive English courses, which helped him land a role in the box-office (5) .... hit *Philadelphia* in 1993.

However, success for Banderas came at a (6) .... His personal life became public when he fell in love with co-star Melanie Griffith from the film *Two Much*. Gossip (7) .... across the country were filled with news about the (8) .... of his eight-year marriage to a Spanish actress. Banderas insisted that his marriage had been at risk for some time and said of Griffith, 'I love this woman, and I want to make her happy – that is my only purpose.'

0 A unhesitating	B undoubting	C undeniable	D unanswerable
1 A embarked	B diverged	C undertook	D propelled
2 A discovered	B founded	C initiated	D starred
3 A voice	B provide	C exhibit	D express
4 A realised	B proved	C made	D came
5 A breaking	B rush	C smash	D crash
6 A fee	B penalty	C cost	D price
7 A columns	B articles	C features	D editorials
8 A break	B downfall	C breakup	D destruction

2 For questions 1–8, read the text below and think of the word which best fits each gap. Use only one word in each gap. There is an example at the beginning (0).

Seeking fame and fortune

Young people who choose professions such as acting or singing invariably sacrifice a great deal (0) ......__if__...... if they are to achieve their goal. Their parents often organise for (1) .... to have special coaching in singing, acting and so on in addition to their conventional schooling. This way of life is similar to (2) .... of young athletes. Their school grades may suffer (3) .... a result of the drive to become stars.

(4) .... they reach their late teens and early 20s, these youngsters travel from audition to audition in the hope of (5) .... spotted by some famous director or producer. And a few become mega-stars, some make a decent living out of their profession and others may give (6) .... their ambition because they never get a lucky break.

Taking all this (7) .... consideration, it is hard to imagine that anyone who does become a celebrity could possibly resent media attention and the adulation of their fans.

This is (8) .... I believe superstars' complaints about media harassment are often just another publicity stunt.

4 Acting on advice

Use of English

1 For questions 1–8, read the article and decide which answer
(A, B, C or D) best fits each gap.

Be careful
what you buy

When choosing hi-fi equipment, it is important to choose a retailer carefully. Independent hi-fi shops have (0) _knowledgeable_ staff who can demonstrate equipment before a purchase is made. However, retailers that lack demonstration rooms should not be ignored, as they often have another (1) .... that has them. Chain stores are worth considering as they offer good prices and some also have reasonable demonstration (2) .... Then, there are 'ex-demo models', which can save money if the hi-fi is merely scratched, but purchasers should beware of retailers using the term to try and sell returned or (3) .... equipment. The best advice is to look for shops advertising membership of an Audio Dealers' Association, because they have to (4) .... to certain standards of conduct.

In general, unauthorised dealers are best (5) .... because they may be getting the products from a third party, which can cause problems later with warranties. Extended warranties can make (6) .... in some cases but may not always be good value for money. When a product is offered at an extremely low price, purchasers should check carefully that the (7) .... and conditions, as well as the price, are realistic and that there is a manufacturer's full warranty. Another source to be wary of is 'grey imports' (imported through unofficial channels). These can appear good value, but also have (8) .... when it comes to warranties and servicing.

0	**A** acclaimed	**B** knowledgeable	**C** influential	**D** compatible
1	**A** branch	**B** offshoot	**C** section	**D** domain
2	**A** abilities	**B** faculties	**C** facilities	**D** aptitudes
3	**A** waste	**B** substandard	**C** dead	**D** failed
4	**A** stay	**B** hold	**C** attach	**D** adhere
5	**A** eluded	**B** avoided	**C** evaded	**D** abandoned
6	**A** meaning	**B** significance	**C** sense	**D** reason
7	**A** terms	**B** formats	**C** points	**D** clauses
8	**A** inconveniences	**B** fears	**C** drawbacks	**D** troubles

Listening

1 **[1] [05]** You will hear a third-year university student called Franco giving advice to school leavers about choosing a university. For questions 1–8, complete the sentences.

Choosing a university

Franco's parents advised him to reconsider his first choice of university because of its
(1) ....
At a university open day, talking to
(2) .... helped Franco get a good understanding of student life there.
Franco advises reading the **(3)** .... carefully before choosing a course.
Franco was impressed by the **(4)** .... one tutor at his university had written.
Franco was able to compare online the
(5) .... in different university cities.
Franco was glad that he had looked into
(6) .... possibilities in the area around his university.

According to Franco, many students don't find out about the **(7)** .... at the university they are interested in going to. Franco says that it's worth checking out the types of **(8)** .... available for first-year students.

Vocabulary

1 In the listening, there was an example of the prefix *over-* in *overview*. What do the words in bold mean?

1 You can read an **overview** of the situation on our website. ....
2 Don't be tempted to study **overnight** before the exam. ....
3 My father works **overseas**. ....
4 The sky looks **overcast**. ....
5 You'll find the summary **overleaf** on page 12. ....
6 You shouldn't **overeat**. ....
7 Sorry I completely forgot about it. It was an **oversight**. ....

2 In the recording, you heard the phrase *tighten your belt*, which means you have to economise because you don't have much money. This suffix *-en* is added to words to make verbs which mean 'become more'. Use the words in the box and add *-en* to complete these sentences.

broad	tight	strength	wide
length	thick	straight	white

1 They are going to .... the road as it has become too narrow for the volume of traffic which uses it.
2 She stood up and .... her crumpled clothes.
3 We're all going to have to .... our belts until the economic situation improves.
4 I'll have to .... this skirt – it's too short to wear to work.
5 You can .... the sauce if it's too thin by adding some flour.
6 The rise in interest rates has caused the dollar to ....
7 They say that travel .... the mind.
8 She's going to ask the dentist to .... her teeth, but I don't think they look discoloured.

3 In the listening, you heard an irregular plural: *criteria* (the singular noun is *criterion*). What is the plural of these singular nouns?

1 leaf ....

2 fish ....

3 series ....

4 passer-by ....

5 analysis ....

6 half ....

7 stimulus ....

8 index ....

9 medium ....

10 self ....

Modals and semi-modals (1)

1 Match each modal verb in bold to the uses in the box.

permission   order   ability   request
theoretical possibility   negative certainty

1 I **can** speak four languages. ....

2 That **can't** be his brother. He looks nothing like him! ....

3 You **can** sit here if you want. ....

4 You made the mess, so you **can** clear it up. ....

5 **Could** you pass me the dictionary? ....

6 **Can** this software be installed on any computer? ....

2 Complete these sentences with the correct form of *can*, *could* or *might*.

1 Carol .... eat the meal I'd cooked because she's allergic to seafood.

2 .... you use tinned tomatoes for this recipe?

3 He .... gone on holiday – I've just seen him in the city centre.

4 .... you help me with these boxes, please?

5 That woman .... be his wife, but as I've never seen her, I'm not sure.

6 My sister .... be able to make it to the party but we're not sure.

7 We've been waiting for an hour – you .... let us know you'd be late.

8 It .... be a genuine diamond, but it's highly unlikely.

3 Complete the sentences using the correct form of the words in brackets.

1 I .... find any fresh figs in the shop so I used dried ones instead. (be able to)

2 How many words .... write for the assignment? (I have to)

3 He .... two photos for his passport application. (need)

4 We got off the bus at the wrong stop and .... walk for miles. (have to)

5 I'm sorry I'm busy right now but I .... help you in about 10 minutes. (should)

6 You .... bought any more apples. There are plenty in the fruit bowl. (need)

4 Advanced learners often make mistakes with the word order of modals. Find the mistakes in three of these sentences and correct them.

1 You either should buy a bike or a motorbike.

....

2 You can either catch a local train or use the Underground.

....

3 But you can still make delicious food, for yourself and for others.

....

4 You have only to remember to enrol for the exam at least a month before.

....

5 I need always to keep up with the latest news.

....

G → Student's Book page 163

Dream jobs

Relative clauses

1 You saw this advertisement, and you are interested in replying to it.
You have written some notes in preparation for your letter of application.
Rewrite the notes into longer sentences using relative clauses.

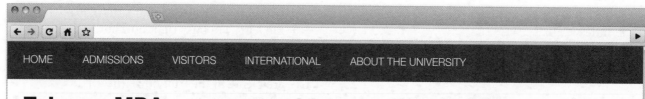

| HOME | ADMISSIONS | VISITORS | INTERNATIONAL | ABOUT THE UNIVERSITY |

Take an MBA – a passport to your dream job

You can start our Distance Learning MBA programme at any time, wherever you are based. If you're ready for a world-class management degree, you could start as early as next week.

We are one of the country's leading business schools, providing one of the most effective routes to an MBA, with more than 2,000 successful graduates from over 80 countries.

One of the reasons for our popularity is that we offer flexibility and an affordable fee structure. Our challenging courses are not easy, however, and you will need to hold a good degree in a relevant subject area. However, no prior knowledge of business administration is required. During the course, you will be working at your own pace.

Our high standards are maintained by the expertise of our teaching faculty and a first-class reputation stemming from our truly international perspective.

Click here for further information or an application form.

1 I am writing – MBA. I understand it starts any time.
....
....

2 I would like to start September. I return from annual holiday.
....
....

3 I would like to take course in my home country. I will have access to internet and good libraries.
....
....
....

4 I graduated from ... two years ago. Studied Politics and Economics. BSc Honours degree.
....
....

5 I am employed by plastics, Wisbro. Sales and Marketing department.
....
....

6 You can obtain reference from Sven Larsson. Marketing manager. Worked closely with him for two years.
....
....

G→ Student's Book page 164

2 ⊙ The *Cambridge English Corpus* shows that advanced learners often make mistakes with relative clauses. Correct these sentences written by exam candidates.

1 There were about 15 students who was selected to participate in this programme.
....

2 I couldn't meet my friend Ann, who live in St Andrews.
....

3 I hope that everyone who want to take the test will pass it.
....

4 The opening hours are 8 am to 10 pm, what is perfect for all the students.
....

5 More ingredients from different seasons are used together, what provides more variety.
....

6 I do not know where have you found the information.
....

7 You can also go to the Tourist Board to see what are the places to visit.
....

8 I would be very pleased if I could receive a written notification about what is the company going to do.
....

9 Many people can't imagine what would life be like without their car.
....

10 Don't you remember what was Denise's wedding like?
....

11 The book explains to us what are the challenges for the next century.
....

12 Of course, there are still women which stop working at the time they marry.
....

Writing

1 Write a letter in response to the information below in 220–260 words in an appropriate style. Before you write, think about these points.

• Who are you writing to?
• Why are you writing?
• What style of language is suitable?
• What information do you need to include?
• What do you hope will happen as a result of your letter?

> The international company you work for is expanding its office in London. It would like to attract employees from different countries. You have been asked by your manager to write a letter to an online recruitment agency. Your letter should explain the type of work your company is involved in and the advantages of working for your company. You should also explain what qualities you are looking for in suitable applicants.

Listening

1 🔊 1 06 You will hear five short extracts in which tour guides are talking about their jobs. While you listen, you must complete both tasks.

Task 1

Choose from the list (A–H) the difficulty each speaker experienced in their job at first.

A learning a new language
B the weather
C the lack of privacy
D organising transport
E the unsociable hours
F the demands of the tourists
G perceived lack of security
H changing diet

Speaker 1 ☐
Speaker 2 ☐
Speaker 3 ☐
Speaker 4 ☐
Speaker 5 ☐

Task 2

Choose from the list (A–H) what each speaker appreciates most about their job.

A doing a range of tasks
B being treated as a local
C having unexpected experiences
D the uniqueness of the landscape
E discovering information
F being part of a team
G going to rarely seen places
H overcoming obstacles

Speaker 1 ☐
Speaker 2 ☐
Speaker 3 ☐
Speaker 4 ☐
Speaker 5 ☐

Reading

1 You are going to read extracts from the blogs of four trainee lawyers. For questions 1–10, choose from the blogs (A–D). The blogs may be chosen more than once.

Which trainee lawyer

1 finds aspects of the work mentally exhausting?
2 would like to take on more responsibility?
3 realises they have a financial advantage?
4 has no regular pattern to the working day?
5 accepts the limitations of what they can do?
6 enjoys the financial security of the job?
7 likes working with high-profile clients?
8 values the after-work socialising?
9 appreciates being treated as an equal?
10 has difficulties fulfilling one task in detail?

A
I have wanted to be a lawyer for a long, long time, but I didn't always think I would want to be a solicitor. Until my first year in university, I wanted to be a barrister, but even then I could see it is a very financially insecure occupation. As a solicitor, you are more stable because you're someone's employee.

I get in to work every day at about 9.15 in the morning, but there isn't a particular routine after that. I work in employment law. I can't really structure my day because I'm at the beck and call of people above me in the department. I have to be ready to assist them with whatever they are working on and of course what I can do at this early stage of my career is quite restricted.

B
I do enjoy my job mainly because there is a great deal of interaction with the rest of the team. I join the regular meetings where cases are discussed in detail and everyone talks to me in exactly the same way as they do everyone else, even though I've only been here as a trainee for a few months. I'd really like to stay on here after my probationary period.

When our work involves employees who are subject to disciplinary action because of their conduct, things can get emotionally stressful though. It's surprising how many really well-known companies don't actually treat their employees very well. When I go home all I want to do is put my feet up and watch TV. Still, I know this is what I want to do and after six months I'll have a pay review and I'm looking forward to that.

C
As a trainee, obviously you don't have complete control over specific cases and files. However, there are some areas that I feel I'm in charge of – if I can put it like that – for example, drafting letters and amending contracts. Even then everything is checked by a much more experienced lawyer. I'm sure I could take on much more though. After all, that's how you learn – by actually doing the work.

There's a lot of attending meetings, too. As a trainee you don't contribute all that much at these but you do take word-for-word attendance notes, which can be a bit boring and is a nightmare because you can never get everything down. Still, as a trainee I finish my working day at around 6 o'clock but I know many of the lawyers in this firm work until nine at least two evenings a week. It's a pity as that means there isn't really what I'd describe as a social culture here.

D
The money is enough to live on. I'm lucky, mind you, because I live at home and so I don't have to pay rent. I have one major holiday a year and a few weekends away as well.

I enjoy working in London – I think you get interesting work; cases that may involve famous people and are reported on national and international news. My supervisor is very careful about how much responsibility to give me – she can judge when I'm reaching my maximum workload and eases up on how much she's giving me for a while.

I like going for a drink with the others when we've finished work, which I don't think exists everywhere. It has helped me get to know everyone much more quickly, I think. But I'm pretty sure it would be a struggle to afford to do the things I want to do if I had to pay for my own place to live here.

6 Connections

Listening

1 **1|07** Listen to the talk about text messaging and complete the notes.

Some people **(1)** .... at the non-standard language used in texts.

The message the speaker says you might send from a bus is **(2)** ....

Text messages use abbreviations partly because they were limited to **(3)** .... characters.

By 2008 more than **(4)** .... text messages had been sent.

Text messaging became available to the public in **(5)** ....

The speaker gives examples of text messaging being used by religious leaders, **(6)** .... and shops.

People wanting to start a relationship feel that a text message is not as **(7)** .... as a phone call.

It has been observed that the literacy of **(8)** .... is not as good as it used to be.

One person believes that the language of text messages helps the language to **(9)** .... rather than destroying it.

IMO stands for **(10)** ....

An abbreviation that must have caused problems is **(11)** ....

Text messages could be said to have replaced **(12)** .... as the way that lovers communicate.

2 Add the verbs from the box to make phrases from the listening.

> make (x3)   have (x3)   catch (x2)

1 .... the point that
2 slow to .... on
3 to .... someone off guard
4 .... an impact on something
5 .... an argument
6 .... contact
7 .... an effect on something
8 .... the effort

3 Complete these sentences with the correct form of phrases from exercise 2.

1 My uncle isn't very technically minded, but even he has now .... to learn how to send emails.
2 The professor has long .... that watching too much television might .... a negative .... children's literacy skills.
3 Kate hates any kind of conflict and would do anything to avoid ....
4 It must have been very romantic when he .... with her by sending those flowers.
5 Watching TV online was .... but now everyone seems to do it.
6 Tamara had no idea Sam liked her, so she was completely .... when he asked her out.

Phrasal verbs (1)

1 Add one word to each gap.

1 Sorry, I'm calling from the station and it's very noisy here. Can you speak ....?

2 I was just about to apologise for forgetting to meet her after work when she hung .... on me.

3 Just a minute, we're going into a tunnel. I'm breaking .... I'll call you .... later.

4 I'll have to go. My battery's running .... I'll phone you .... later.

5 It was lovely to talk to you. Hang .... a moment. I'll just pass you .... to your dad. He'd like a word with you.

6 I've been trying to ring my uncle but I can't get .... to him.

7 You'd like to speak to the Managing Director? One moment, sir. I'll put you ....

2 Complete the conversations with the correct form of verbs from the boxes.

give in   hand in   look up   pad out
look through

Alexa: Have you finished your project work?

Nick: Not quite. I still need to **(1)** .... a few references in the library. I'm planning to **(2)** .... it .... on Monday. Is yours finished?

Alexa: Well, I finished mine last night. But when I **(3)** .... it .... this morning, I realised it's a bit short and I need to **(4)** .... it .... a bit. So, I'll probably .... mine **(5)** .... on Monday too.

book into   get in   see off   stop over
touch down

Paulo: We **(6)** .... my sister .... at the airport yesterday. She's gone on holiday to New Zealand for a couple of weeks.

Rosa: Lucky her! Did she go on a direct flight?

Paulo: No, she **(7)** .... in Dubai on the way there. In fact her plane should be **(8)** .... by now, if it is on time.

Rosa: Well, I've flown several times and we always **(9)** .... on time. Has she got friends to stay with?

Paulo: No, she **(10)** .... a nice hotel.

set up   hand in   take on   close down

Sam: How's work these days?

Kate: Well, I'm snowed under, but I suppose that's better than having nothing to do. What about you?

Sam: Well, the company I've been working for **(11)** .... next month and I've got to find something else to do.

Kate: Oh dear.

Sam: Well, I was thinking of **(12)** .... my notice .... anyway. I'm thinking of **(13)** .... my own business.

Kate: That's a great idea. If you ever need to **(14)** .... extra staff, let me know!

G → Student's Book page 165

Vocabulary

1 Choose one word from A and one from B to complete each sentence. Change the form of the verb if you need to.

A	B
do	chance housework favour
have	complaint best seriously
make	mistake time photos
take	nap responsibility effort

1 It doesn't matter whether you win the competition or not. The important thing is to .... your ....

2 Anna .... some wonderful .... on holiday in Scotland last year.

3 I always .... the .... on Saturday mornings so I can have the rest of the weekend free.

4 I thought that was Jo I saw over there, but I must have .... a .... She's in France at the moment.

5 You'll never manage to learn this vocabulary unless you really .... an ....

6 The state of this bathroom is disgusting. I would like to .... an official .... to the hotel manager.

7 I think everyone .... a great .... at the party last night.

8 When she was in Ireland last year, Giovanna made sure she .... every .... she could to speak English.

9 Could you possibly .... me a .... and get me some books from the library while you're there?

10 My grandpa usually .... a .... in the afternoon.

11 Piotr lied about his age because he thought that no one would .... him .... if they knew how young he really was.

12 Now that you are 18, it is really time that you .... a bit more .... for your own finances.

2 The *Cambridge English Corpus* shows that advanced learners often use a wrong verb instead of *do, have, make* and *take*. Correct these sentences written by exam candidates.

1 We simply want to spend a nice time together.

....

2 I passed such a good time in Chile.

....

3 If you take any problems, call me at the hotel.

....

4 We do not have time to take a full meal during the lunch break.

....

5 Why don't we make a barbecue?

....

6 Mobile phones have made a great impact on us.

....

7 There was no social programme at the summer school while I was there, but I found very good friends.

....

8 I think that some changes should be done to improve the museum.

....

9 With some effort, some really great improvements can be done.

....

10 I would also like to express a few suggestions about some different activities.

....

11 They are feeling unhealthy because they don't practise enough sport.

....

12 He had no possibility of entering the exam.

....

3 Choose the correct word in these sentences.

1 Please write to me soon, otherwise I will *make / take* further steps.

2 If you don't pass the exam, you won't *take / get* a certificate.

3 A friend of mine who *did / made* the same course was very happy with it.

4 You may have another chance in the future to *have / take* the same course.

5 I *conducted / made* a survey among the club members.

6 It's very important to *take / attract* young people's attention.

7 You can *go / do* shopping in your spare time.

8 First of all, I *found / had* some difficulties in reaching the hotel.

Reading

1 Read the book review and answer the questions which follow it. Choose the answer (A, B, C or D) which you think fits best according to the text.

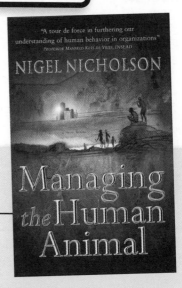

Zoo management

Dylan Evans finds business to be a jungle in
Managing the Human Animal **by Nigel Nicholson**

In the past few years, evolutionary psychology (or EP as it is known) hasn't had much impact in the world of business. However, that may be about to change. A new book by Nigel Nicholson, professor of organisational behaviour at the London Business School, promises to transform EP from an academic theory into a practical tool for management.

According to Nicholson, executives have been misled by decades of utopian management education. They have been encouraged to believe that they can re-engineer their companies in any way they want, eliminating turf wars and sexism along the way. Such fantasies, however, take no account of the enduring features of human nature, which stubbornly resists the new visions imposed upon it. No wonder so many great new management ideas fail as soon as they move from the business school to the boardroom.

The solution, argues Nicholson, is to construct a new approach to management, based on EP. As the first truly scientific account of human nature, EP can teach managers how to work with the grain rather than against it.

Take emotions, for example. A lot of previous management thinking downplayed the role of emotions in decision-making. In line with Plato and a whole host of Western thinkers since, emotions were seen as at best harmless luxuries, and at worst, outright obstacles to rational action. Only recently have managers begun to realise that emotional intelligence is vital to business success. EP provides a firm scientific basis for this new trend in management thinking, seeing emotions as complex mechanisms that can enhance rationality in the right circumstances. As Nicholson explains in a fascinating chapter on 'playing the rationality game', managers who view emotions – in themselves or in their workforce – as mere obstacles are wasting one of their greatest potential resources.

Nicholson's prose is pacy and down-to-earth, and he illustrates the main ideas of EP and their relevance to the business world with well-chosen examples, such as risk-taking and the context of biology. As Nicholson notes, zoologists have often observed that the closer an animal gets to the survival boundary, the more chances it will take to secure vital resources.

Such comparisons with animal behaviour will no doubt enrage those who think that all scientific claims should be hedged with multiple caveats and disclaimers. On the other hand, for those who are fed up with repeated calls for 'safe science' and other forms of political correctness, Nicholson's pragmatic view is refreshing. He takes a theory that has been neither effectively established nor conclusively refuted, and advises managers to try it out. A theory may sometimes be tested more decisively in the crucible of business than in the science laboratory.

EP may not get tested at all any more, unless it is used to shape policy and corporate strategy. There is currently a small but vociferous group of academics who proclaim that EP is so fundamentally flawed that further testing is superfluous. It can, moreover, lead you to become a genetic determinist and, even worse, a reductionist. The very possibility of such a terrible fate is enough to strike fear into the minds of many liberal intellectuals, and dissuade them from putting EP to further scientific tests. Thankfully, however, these philosophical worries are not usually uppermost in the average manager's mind. Executives are more often worried about more mundane matters, such as the figures on the bottom line. And so, even if EP is denied a fair hearing in the dining rooms of the intelligentsia, it may get a better chance in the boardroom.

It would be premature, then, and most unscientific, to prejudge Nicholson's hypothesis. Whether he is right, or whether his own brand of management thinking will go the same way as those he decries, only time will tell. If the managers who take on board the ideas of EP perform better than those who don't, Nicholson's gambit will have paid off.

1 Nicholson believes that executives in the past
  A were given an unrealistic view of their own powers.
  B paid little attention to management theory.
  C failed to listen to their own members of staff.
  D wanted to introduce change too rapidly.

2 What does Nicholson present as the strength of his argument?
  A It brings together business theories.
  B It is based on scientific research into business behaviour.
  C It is rooted in management experience.
  D It takes human nature into full consideration.

3 The writer suggests that a reading of Plato encouraged later Western thinkers
  A to exaggerate the importance of emotional intelligence.
  B to feel that philosophy has little relevance for business life.
  C to believe that emotions and rationalism are in opposition to each other.
  D to see emotions as complex to interpret.

4 What point is made in the fifth paragraph regarding Nicholson's approach?
  A He uses scientific terminology.
  B He writes using a clear and easy style.
  C He deals with his subject matter in a superficial way.
  D He only presents examples that support his point of view.

5 What point is the writer making when he compares the dining rooms of the intelligentsia to the boardroom?
  A Academics may be less open-minded than business people about the possibilities of EP.
  B The intelligentsia are more likely than managers to think about EP.
  C Academics and business people should work together to develop management theories.
  D The intelligentsia are less aware of the realities of the business world than managers are.

6 What is the reviewer's conclusion about Nicholson's hypothesis?
  A It is a radical and important contribution to the theory of management.
  B It needs to be tried out in practice before judgement can be made about it.
  C It represents another trend which is likely to lose its appeal with time.
  D It is less soundly and scientifically based than Nicholson claims it to be.

Reason, result and purpose

1 **Rewrite each sentence using the word in brackets. There may be more than one possible answer.**

1 The business is experiencing some problems because oil prices have recently risen. (result)

....

2 The company's difficulties have come about thanks to some poor decisions made last year. (stem)

....

3 Owing to the delays to the CEO's flight, the meeting began much later than expected. (consequence)

....

4 Installing a new software system has caused some initial problems for staff. (resulted)

....

5 I hope my absence next week won't create any difficulties for the company. (rise)

....

6 As we were slow to take advantage of new technologies, we've fallen behind our competitors. (due)

....

7 Jason has a lot of experience in exports and so the company was keen to recruit him. (as)

....

G → Student's Book page 166

Writing

1 **Do the writing task below.**

You see this announcement in an international magazine.

In their late teens, young people have to make a big decision: to stay in education or go straight to work. What factors affect this decision in your country? To what extent has the proportion of young people choosing to go straight into work changed in your country? What developments in society have influenced this change? Please send us a report about the situation in your country.

Write a **report** in 220–260 words.

Reading and Use of English

1 For questions 1–8, read the text and then decide which word best fits each gap.

Improving the business process

Improving business is the ultimate aim of any company's operations. Improvements translate directly to better (0) ....*profits*.... by reducing expenditure and increasing competitiveness at the same time. If an insurance company, for instance, can underwrite policies or (1) .... claims faster, it can provide better service, compete better with smaller online competitors, and (2) .... costs, which again helps it to compete. Unfortunately, any company has a limited amount of money to spend on business process improvement, and those in charge of budgets have to (3) .... carefully. If the IT department (4) .... the choice, new hardware, software, applications, etc. would be installed. The HR department would hire better qualified people, (5) .... them with more training, and have a better working environment. However, practical considerations always force companies to (6) .... and choose the best things to spend money on. But how does anyone know that a training course on people skills will actually (7) .... a difference to customer satisfaction? This is where a system of process modelling with cause-and-effect analysis (8) .... in. It can help any company make the best decisions possible.

0 A expenses	**B** profits	C charges	D overheads
1 A agree	B cope	C settle	D deal
2 A cut	B break	C weaken	D decline
3 A prioritise	B guess	C control	D list
4 A wanted	B had	C kept	D set
5 A provide	B offer	C introduce	D enhance
6 A take	B pick	C decide	D get
7 A do	B work	C make	D see
8 A walks	B goes	C comes	D gets

Being inventive

Reading and Use of English

1 Complete each gap in the blog with one word.

I am at a conference. (0) ...*Every*...... seat has a power outlet, microphone for questions and voting buttons for group participation. I can see over 80 laptops or tablets scattered (1) .... the room, with only a handful of people using paper and pens. As (2) .... as I can tell, at least 20 people in the audience are busy checking their emails, about ten are writing documents, and the rest seem to be surfing the web. The current presenter is using all the technology to give an overview of yet (3) .... new business model. But this model is not novel and his delivery is boring, so I walk to the back of the room (4) .... a cup of coffee. This speaker has been wasting his own time and (5) .... of everyone else in the room. However, people are listening with one ear, while getting (6) .... with productive activities. At (7) ...., the speaker gets to the punch line, receives a round of applause, and retires. I return to my seat and start writing these words as the next speaker sets up. I relax in the knowledge that I can continue working and thinking, irrespective (8) .... the quality of the remaining presentations.

2 Read the text below. Use the word given in capitals at the end of some of the lines to form a word that fits in the gap in the same line.

Human inventiveness

Humans are a species possessing great (0) .... *ingenuity* ....   **INGENIOUS**
From the moment someone made the first sharp-edged tool, to the development of Mars rovers and the internet, several key
(1) .... stand out as particularly   **ADVANCE**
(2) .... Here is what we think is the most important   **REVOLUTION**
invention of all time.
Some people may argue that other contenders are more
(3) ...., but for us it's the light bulb that gets the   **DESERVE**
prize. After all, when all you have is natural light, people's
(4) .... is limited to daylight hours. Light bulbs   **PRODUCE**
changed the world by allowing us to be active at night. According
to one of our leading (5) ...., two dozen people   **HISTORY**
were instrumental in inventing incandescent lamps; Thomas Edison,
however receives (6) .... as the primary inventor   **RECOGNISE**
because he created a completely functional lighting system,
including a generator and wiring as well as a carbon-filament bulb.
As well as initiating the introduction of electricity in homes
throughout the world, this invention also had rather an
(7) .... consequence of changing people's sleep   **EXPECT**
patterns. Instead of going to bed at nightfall and sleeping for
periods throughout the night separated by times of being
(8) ...., we now stay up except for the 7–8 hours   **WAKE**
allotted for sleep, and, ideally, sleep all in one go.

Modals and semi-modals (2)

1 Look at the photo of the inventor and the sentences about him. Choose the correct words for each sentence.

1 The man in the photo *used to / used* love designing unusual machines when he was a child.

2 He *would / should* spend hours first drawing and then building his designs.

3 His teachers were impressed by his original ideas and suggested he *shall / should* become an inventor when he grew up.

4 They advised him that if he wanted to be a successful inventor he *had to / must to* have a good understanding of science.

5 So he decided he *would / ought* study physics at university.

6 However, once he got to university, he realised he *should have / must have* chosen to do engineering.

7 It *must have / had to have* been quite difficult for him but he changed courses in the middle of his first year at university.

8 After graduating, he got a job in a large company but soon decided he *must / should* be working more independently.

9 So he left his job and started working on his own – he's *had to / must* work very hard but he's becoming very successful.

10 He does a lot of work in his kitchen at home although his wife says he *ought / should* to build himself a shed in their garden.

2 ⊙ The *Cambridge English Corpus* shows that advanced learners often use the wrong modal verb. Add *should, would,* or *could* to these sentences.

1 First, it .... be better to avoid busy periods.

2 Also, you .... pay us a little more if we work harder.

3 Large parking areas .... be provided next to the subway, otherwise people won't be able to park.

4 It .... be a good idea to avoid mentioning the bad news.

5 When you visit our country, you .... visit the lakes and go swimming any time.

G → Student's Book page 166

Reading

1 Read articles A–F and answer the questions.

1 Which articles relate to health issues?
.... , ...

2 Which article is about education? ....

3 Which article is about the US? ....

4 Which article is about sailing? ....

5 Which article focuses on a positive change? ....

6 Which article focuses on a negative trend? ....

7 Which articles have a clear political focus?
.... , ...

8 Which articles are concerned with prizes?
.... , ...

A

Making progress for the future

There will be few in the corporate world who don't realise that marketing and innovation are key factors behind successful business. However, decision-makers in the European Union are only just becoming aware of this fact, according to one senior management expert.

B

A matter of time

Whether people are learning online or in classrooms, one thing is for sure – IT skills are more desirable than ever. Yet in the busy workplace, employees are finding they have less time than ever, especially when it comes to training themselves in new technologies.

C

'Northern Innovation' in front position

The Oceans Race, the non-stop competition to be fastest to circumnavigate the globe, has upped its pace after a slow start to the contest last week. In first place yesterday was the 100-foot yacht, Northern Innovation, piloted by Rachel Jackson, and Steven Barnstaple. Having covered 1,200 kilometres in a no-holds-barred five days at sea, she has now reached the port of Dubai.

D

The new national website from the National Childbirth Trust has proved so innovative, it is winning awards. The website allows parents to gain information about childbirth, as well as to get support and access to expert counsellors quickly and efficiently. Up-to-date links allow parents to find their nearest local expert.

E

Ancient Greece would not have been the best place to get sick. Standards of public sanitation might have been world-beating at the time, and scientific understanding unrivalled – but nowhere near the standards of even the most dilapidated public hospitals you can find today.

F

Stalking the corridors of power

Washington swarms with a thousand industrial lobbyists. They lurk around the extravagant restaurants and offices which stretch from the White House to the Capitol building – a two-mile axis along which money and power are constantly traded.

2 Read the articles again. Find words or phrases that have a positive or a negative connotation.

positive	negative
brand new	old hat

Listening

1 🔊 **1.08** Listen to a talk about innovation in education. Complete the gaps with one or two words.

Online courses are sometimes considered attractive because colleges think they are
(1) .... and students think they are less hard work.
The speaker is sceptical about these ideas because of her years of experience as a
(2) .... of online courses.
The speaker recommends students go through a
(3) .... in using the software before starting to prepare an online course.
Students should put a
(4) .... in a prominent position and should check their online course space daily.
Research has highlighted how important friendly
(5) .... with their fellow students is for online students.
The speaker says that introducing yourself to your tutor may make him or her feel that you have good
(6) ....
The speaker says that some online students get into problems because of
(7) ....

2 Here are some words and phrases from the talk. Are they used here with a positive (P) or a negative (N) connotation?

1 money-saving ....
2 succinct ....
3 considerate ....
4 eager ....
5 lengthy ....
6 consumed ....

9 Urban living

Listening

1 🔊**1 09** You hear a discussion of megacities between two students, Maria and Dan. Answer the questions.

1 How much experience do the students have of living in megacities?
   A Maria has more experience of life in a megacity than Dan has.
   B Dan has spent more time in a megacity than Maria has.
   C They have both spent a similar period of time living in a megacity.

2 What problem with life in New York does Dan consider to be most significant?
   A the noise and pollution of the city
   B the time wasted on travelling every day
   C the relative lack of a sense of community

2 🔊**1 10** You hear a man telling his friend about his decision to move to the countryside. Answer the questions.

1 The man is considering moving out of the city because he wants to
   A have more living space.
   B develop a new interest.
   C please his family.

2 What does the man say he would miss about city life?
   A good public transport
   B varied entertainment
   C plentiful shops

3 🔊**1 11** You hear two friends discussing how their city, Stowton, has changed. Answer the questions.

1 The friends agree that
   A the city is typical of other places of a similar size.
   B the city planners have had to take some difficult decisions.
   C a geographical feature has had a negative impact on the city's growth.

2 The woman feels that most of the changes to their city
   A are for the better.
   B have failed to improve it.
   C have both positive and negative aspects.

4 Match the words in the box with phrases 1–10 to make collocations from the recordings.

have	gap	bump	pass	raise
be	come	take	traffic	give

1 .... objections
2 .... permission
3 .... round to an idea
4 .... an impact
5 .... in someone else's shoes
6 .... into someone you know
7 .... the time of day
8 .... some getting used to
9 .... congestion
10 .... year

Writing

1 Do the writing task below.

The local council of the town where you live has invited residents to submit proposals about how to improve the town centre. The proposal should include suggestions relating to leisure facilities, shopping and transport. Your suggestions may be as radical as you wish but you must explain clearly why you feel they would benefit residents.

Write your **proposal** in 220–260 words.

Future forms

1 Read these statements about city development plans. Underline all the different ways in which the writer refers to the future.

'They're currently building lots of new blocks of flats to the east of the city. I'm going to try to rent one of them when they're ready next year. I hope it may be a bit cheaper than living in the centre – as I do at present – as rents here are really high.'

'Central government considers it imperative that those who are in charge of writing city development plans should place the main emphasis on what will happen, where it will happen and why it will happen.'

'The planning system aims to lend its backing to proposals that will contribute to sustainable economic growth.'

'It goes without saying that all future city development plans should do their utmost to protect and enhance the natural environment but they will also simultaneously have to maintain people's access to open space and recreation opportunities.'

'50 new three- and four-bedroom houses will be built on a site ten kilometers to the north of the city centre. These will be in easy reach of local shops, schools and leisure facilities and are likely to be snapped up by young families.'

'They'll soon have completed the construction of a new block of flats at the end of our street and the apartments there will be going on sale there in the next few weeks. We're going to have to put up with a lot more traffic congestion in the area, I suspect.'

2 Answer these questions about the way future concepts are expressed in English, based on the examples you underlined in exercise 1.

  1 Which future form is more common in the statements: *will* or *going to*? Why is this form more common in this context?

  2 What modal forms are used in the statements to express a future idea?

G → Student's Book page 167

Vocabulary

1 Match phrases 1–10 with a word or expression from the statements. There are two phrases for each speaker.

  1 at the moment: ....

  2 not far from: ....

  3 bought without hesitation: ....

  4 have responsibility for: ....

  5 available for purchase: ....

  6 tolerate: ....

  7 support: ....

  8 act as a factor in promoting: ....

  9 try very hard to: ....

  10 at the same time: ....

Reading and Use of English

1 Read the text and choose which word best fits each gap.

> ### Where Glenfield Students Live
>
> In the last 50 years, students, (0) ....*attending*... one of the two universities in the city of Glenfield have opted to live in the suburbs rather than the centre. However, the situation is now changing. Information just released shows there has been a (1) .... in the number of students living in the outskirts of the city, despite the fact that these areas have large numbers of old houses (2) .... into shared flats, the sort of accommodation where students (3) .... to live.
>
> In contrast, the number of students living in the centre of Glenfield has (4) .... up, increasing by 35 % over the last three years. The only two other areas of the city which saw a rise in the number of students living there were Northholt and Seaton – but the rises were small at just 2% (5) .... Glenfield Residents Association, which (6) .... the interests of people who live in the area, have (7) .... the trend. They have reported that the (8) .... of students on the city centre has generally been extremely positive, giving it fresh energy and a livelier atmosphere.

0 A presenting	**B** participating	**C** attending	**D** assisting
1 A loss	**B** break	**C** descent	**D** drop
2 A adjusted	**B** converted	**C** transferred	**D** relocated
3 A incline	**B** tend	**C** enjoy	**D** favour
4 A beaten	**B** fired	**C** blown	**D** shot
5 A respectively	**B** comparatively	**C** effectively	**D** accordingly
6 A illustrates	**B** characterises	**C** represents	**D** signifies
7 A cheered	**B** welcomed	**C** greeted	**D** congratulated
8 A force	**B** consequence	**C** power	**D** impact

2 Complete the second sentence so that it has a similar meaning to the first sentence, using the word given. Do not change the given word. You must use between three and six words including the word given.

1 James was very impressed by how beautiful the city was.
STRONG
The city's ......*beauty made a strong impression on*...... James.

2 The report concluded that permission to extend the house should not be given.
CONCLUSION
The report considering the request for a house
.... that permission should not be given.

3 Why did the city grow so rapidly in the 19th century?
REASON
What was .... of the city in the 19th century?

4 It took a long time to persuade Kate's husband to move to the city.
COME
Kate's husband took a long time to ....
moving to the city.

5 There is much less congestion in the city centre now than there used to be.
AS
The city centre is nothing .... used to be.

6 Jack is really in a very difficult situation at the moment – I don't envy him.
SHOES
I would hate .... at the moment.

You live and learn

Reading

1 Read the article and choose the best answer for questions 1–5 on page 32.

It's true what they say – 'you live and learn'.

Once upon a time, my dream for the future was a fast car and no cooking or cleaning. Having a husband certainly wasn't part of it. But then … I decided to ask my husband to marry me. Let me try to explain what happened.

I never wanted to get married. I really didn't. So the fact that last year I actually proposed to my boyfriend is possibly the most inconsistent thing I have ever done. It is such a U-turn, in fact, that I would not be surprised now if I started voting for a completely different political party, tucking into large steaks or wearing furs and strings of pearls (though I'd like to hope that someone would have the heart to restrain me).

But there it is. I did it, unromantically, one drizzly Monday night outside the pub at closing time. I hadn't planned it. It just sort of came out. It's strange how simple it was to say, though it took me days to get over the shock of having done it. For my voting preferences, vegetarianism and dislike of killing animals for our own vanity are relatively new aspects of me, compared with my antipathy to marriage which dates back almost as far as the cradle, way before the bubbling up of any feminist consciousness. In the early days, it was quite simple: like many sensible five-year-old girls, I hated boys. They were rough, uncivilised creatures and, frankly, they smelled. My favourite childhood game was pretending to be a witch. In that world, boys got turned into frogs.

Later, things got more complicated. As a young teenager, from my limited perspective, I saw two types of women: those who'd stayed at home and raised kids, and those who'd invested in a business suit. I'm afraid to say I most certainly wanted to be in the second camp, at least partly because my mother was a member of the first and, in my straightforward, unpleasant teenage way, I was truly horrified by almost everything my parents did.

In those days, I envisioned a future in which I did no housework (with which my mother seemed to be ceaselessly occupied). Having a husband to iron shirts for certainly wasn't a part of the plan. Men held you back. (I'm afraid that to this day I can't bear cleaning.)

By the time I was at university I was even more sure that I would never get married. At the place where I studied, for every one woman student there were three men. I was taught by men. I was taught about prime ministers and kings and great thinkers, and they were all men. It seemed absolutely clear to me that life was going to be a fight against the dark forces of patriarchy and marriage was an outmoded institution which, as we learned from speakers at our women's lunches in the dismal college bar, bred domestic violence and fostered organised slavery.

Furthermore, I asked, just what exactly was the point? What was the point of dressing up in a white bridal dress (particularly when white can be so unflattering to someone with hips the size of mine) and walking down the aisle on the arm of your father to be presented like a sacrificial lamb at the altar? What was the point of all that consumption and crippling excess and top-hats-and-tails and patronising best men's speeches when the whole enterprise would, in an alarming number of cases, end in tears, disaster and divorce a few years down the line? What was the point when the best relationship I know, (that of my brother and his partner of now nearly 20 years) was happy without the institution of marriage to bind it?

So what happened?

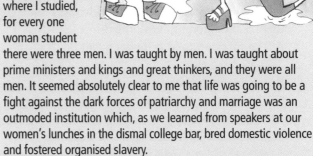

1 What does the writer say would be as out of character for her as her decision to get married?
   A joining a political party
   B buying expensive jewellery
   C wearing old-fashioned clothes
   D eating meat

2 What does the writer say about the origins of her negative feelings about marriage?
   A Her feelings are the result of bad experiences at primary school.
   B She has felt the same way for as long as she can remember.
   C Stories about witches had a very powerful impact on her.
   D She was influenced by the views of other young girls.

3 The writer says her hope for the future, when she was a teenager, was to
   A dress more smartly than her mother.
   B avoid having to do household chores.
   C enjoy a successful business career.
   D have a life more like her father's than her mother's.

4 The writer says that when she was at university
   A her lecturers taught her about feminist theory.
   B she joined a women's activist group.
   C her sense of social injustice was reinforced.
   D she disliked many of the men she met.

5 Why does the writer say she used to feel that there is little point in weddings?
   A The money would be better spent on something else.
   B Not many marriages are successful.
   C The wedding day is often not as good as the couple hoped.
   D Few people look their best at a wedding.

Listening

1 **1.12** **What happened next? Listen and choose the best option for questions 1–4.**

   1 Who first suggested marriage?
   A the writer
   B her parents
   C her boyfriend
   D her brother

2 Why did she change her mind?
   A She was persuaded to by other people.
   B She accepted that marriage was her destiny.
   C She realised she could make her own decisions.
   D She began to see the advantages of being married.

3 Why are the speaker and her boyfriend getting married in a church?
   A They want to please their family and friends.
   B The church is convenient for her home.
   C They have decided they want to do things 'properly'.
   D They like the feeling of historical continuity.

4 Which of these, according to the text, is normally part of a traditional wedding?
   A wearing a veil
   B a Citroën
   C a green dress
   D music from a favourite composer

Vocabulary

1 **Find words and expressions from the article which match these meanings.**

   1 total change in attitude: ....
   2 rainy: ....
   3 awakening: ....
   4 uncomplicated: ....
   5 gloomy: ....
   6 encouraged: ....
   7 eventually: ....

2 **Match these words from the recording to their definitions.**

unromantic   force   make   holy
annoying self-satisfaction   understanding
desire   get married   self-importance   enter

   1 impose ....
   2 cold light of day ....
   3 urge ....
   4 hallowed ....
   5 darken the doors of ....
   6 go up the aisle ....
   7 smugness ....
   8 grasping ....
   9 pomposity ....

3 Complete the table based on words from the reading and listening texts.

Verb	Noun	Adjective
propose	proposal, proposer	proposed
restrain		
		(ir)rational
		simple
invest		
		ceaseless
	slavery	
		sacrificial
suspect		
fail		
–	disaster	
	invention / inventor	
darken		
		formal

4 Complete each sentence with a word from exercise 3.

1 I .... that we wait until the announcement has been made before making a decision.
2 He would like to .... in the property market.
3 Unfortunately, the meeting was a complete .... We didn't agree on anything.
4 The instructions were .... after people complained they were too complicated.
5 I saw a .... looking man standing on the street outside our house.
6 This decision had a .... impact on our country's economy. Everything started to go wrong.
7 She is the most .... person in our team, always thinking up new ideas.

Participle clauses

1 Rewrite these sentences using participle clauses.

1 I did it, unromantically, one drizzly Monday night outside the pub at closing time. I hadn't planned it.

....

....

2 In that world, I was a witch, and boys got turned into frogs.

....

3 Our commitment is already made. In a sense, there is no reason to get married at all.

....

4 But then I began to think about it and to take on board his arguments. I re-examined my objections.

....

5 Once I began to think of marriage as a possible choice out of many possible choices, and not a destiny imposed on me, it didn't seem quite so awful after all.

....

....

6 Once I had got rid of the objections, I started to be able to see certain advantages.

....

....

7 I'm not going for white, but green. I have not darkened the door of a single store's bridal department.

....

....

G → Student's Book page 167

Writing

1 In the article on page 31, the writer's ideas about marriage were affected both by her university years and her childhood experiences. Write a short report on the most important things you have learnt over the last year. Conclude by commenting on the ways in which these things might help you in the future. Write 220–260 words.

Fashion statements

Reading

1 You are going to read an article about computer game use. Six paragraphs have been removed. Choose from the paragraphs A–G the one which fits each gap (1–6).

Trends in gaming

Computer games range from the highly educational and creative to ones with violent-sounding titles such as *World of Warcraft*, designed to lure teenagers and alarm parents. It always worries me to hear the parents of a nine or ten-year-old saying 'He's in his bedroom playing computer games.' And when you ask which games he likes, they do not know. Would these people, if asked who was babysitting, say 'Oh, some guy from the park'?

1

If they are in a kitchen or lounge, parents and older siblings can walk past and keep an eye on what game is being played. They can discuss what the game is about while they are getting on with other activities. Knowing more about what their children enjoy enables parents and children to become closer. Parents should also encourage their children to share gaming with other children. Any game with two or more players is better than one because it promotes discussion. It also dilutes the effect of time spent looking at the screen.

2

It is not only the length of time a child plays computer games for that is important, it is also the time of day they are allowed to play. There is evidence to suggest that playing computer games in the evening can lead to insomnia in some children. They may become too excited and their brain cannot 'switch off'.

3

For this reason, it is recommended that parents install parental control software on their children's phones, so that no matter where they are, what they access is controlled. Most of these software packages record every site visited, and they also filter out games or sites that are unsuitable for the specified age range.

4

Having filtered out games which are too adult for their children, parents have the peace of mind to consider the positives of gaming. Research shows that gaming increases both physical and mental reaction times. Moreover, many games are designed to be educational and require players to do maths and work out complex strategies. Parents should make sure that they review their parental control settings as their children grow up.

5

The best guarantee against damage or confusion is this normal communication parents have with their children. It needs to be maintained even when parents have demanding jobs and children spend much of their time with friends. In fact, modern technology allows parents and children to stay in touch more easily.

6

In the same way, teenagers enjoy being included in their parents' hobbies. Despite the fact that technology is always developing, what good parents do remains surprisingly stable. They love their children and talk to them.

A As children become teenagers they need to be allowed to learn to make their own judgements and become more independent. They will of course make mistakes. Parents will find they have accessed inappropriate sites but as long as a parent is around for long enough, does not overreact, and is willing to listen, then any problems will be resolved.

B Parents should think of gaming as an online playground. If a child plays games online, they may be playing with strangers. Some will be other children and some may be adult enthusiasts. As with any crowd, there will be good people but there also may be some bad ones.

C One way of making sure that parents do know what their children are up to is to keep the computer gaming area in one of the shared parts of the house, for example the sitting room. If children are in their bedrooms, out of sight of the rest of the family, they may be more tempted to access unsuitable games and less likely to ask an adult for permission to download a game.

D This is important because otherwise children may begin to suffer from eyestrain. Children should be told exactly how long they are allowed to browse online for and these limits should be adhered to without exception. Parents should not extend the allowed time just because the children are occupied and not bothering their parents.

E This does not mean that texting or phoning should replace face-to-face communication. Children of all ages enjoy sociable, physical pastimes. We all know that a small child gets more fun out of a sociable kitchen than out of a toy and loves helping dad clean the car more than watching television programme.

F Each video game has a category rating which indicates who the game is suitable for. For example, the symbol EC stands for 'early childhood' and has content intended for young children. E stands for 'everyone' and these games are suitable for all ages and will contain cartoon, mild violence and mild language. Parents need to make sure they understand the rating system so that they can block unsuitable material.

G This lack of sleep can lead to a deterioration of the physical and mental welfare of children, which is the responsibility of their parents. However, it is obvious that they cannot watch over their children every hour of the day. Children can access computer games on mobile devices that they take with them to school; in fact they take smart phones everywhere with them. Parents need to make sure they understand the rating system so that they can block unsuitable material.

Vocabulary

1 Match words in the article with these definitions.

1 attract someone, making them do something they would not normally do: ....
2 brothers or sisters: ....
3 encourage: ....
4 reduce in strength / make weaker: ....
5 put in place: ....
6 look through: ....
7 represent: ....

2 Complete these sentences with words from exercise 1.

1 The shop .... cameras to reduce the amount of theft of high-value designer items.
2 Many people .... markets hoping to find vintage clothes.
3 That blue and green symbol .... fair trade and you find it on all this company's T-shirts.
4 Shoppers were .... into the store by the clever advertising campaign.
5 The newspaper article wanted to .... ethical trade, especially in the fashion industry.

Reported speech

1 In writing, we can use a variety of reporting verbs to introduce reported speech instead of just *say* or *tell*. Choose the correct verb in these sentences. Sometimes both may be possible.

1 He *promised / suggested* to phone me at 9 o'clock.
2 Jane *warned / threatened* me not to touch her computer.
3 I *regretted / insisted* that I should do it myself.
4 She *invited / recommended* them to eat at the Japanese restaurant.
5 He *denied / offered* to sell them to her for a lower price.
6 We *agreed / asked* to see the manager before the end of the month.
7 She *advised / recommended* using the new software.
8 I *told / suggested* her to take an earlier train.

2 Rewrite these statements as reported speech.

> But John, I don't think you should let them use the internet so much. It's not healthy.

1 She advised .... so much.

> I wish we hadn't bought so many computer games.

2 He regretted .... so many computer games.

> Listen Sara, I'll take your laptop away if you leave it switched on it all night.

3 He threatened .... if she left it switched on all night.

> I didn't leave the laptop switched on all night!

4 Sara denied .... all night.

> Yes, it's bad – my children play computer games for at least five hours a day.

5 He complained .... computer games too much.

> If you teach children through physical activities, they can learn a lot.

6 He suggested .... through physical activities.

> Michael, don't stare at the screen for so long – it'll hurt your eyes.

7 Michael's mother warned .... for such a long time.

G → Student's Book page 168

Reading and Use of English

1   For questions 1–8, read the text below. Use the word given in capitals at the end of some of the lines to form a word that fits in the gap in the same line.

The shape of fins to come

Snakeskin might be all the rage in designer
(0) _collections_ this spring, but it could be   **COLLECT**
(1) .... by something even more scaly.   **PLACE**
Several Scandinavian designers have just announced
a new luxury fabric to rival the finest leathers, silks
and furs. No longer will snakeskin, lizard and crocodile
be the (2) .... exotic materials,   **PREFER**
because there's now: fish skin.

A fish leather tannery in Sweden is offering its unique
products to the world's top fashion houses in the hope
that they will scale the (3) .... of chic.   **HIGH**

Turning fish skin into (4) .... dress   **DESIRE**
material is not easy. It takes three days, starting with
a wash to (5) .... most of the fat and dirt.   **MOVE**
The scales are lifted and then the skin is pickled.

'The way we get rid of any (6) .... smell   **OFFEND**
is a secret,' says Bergholz, joint owner of Sea Skin
Scandinavia. Yvonne Eriksson, of the Finnish design
company Fero, (7) ...., is making shirts   **WHILE**
and jackets from fish caught in Lake Victoria, Africa.
'It's a great (8) .... to more traditional   **ALTER**
exotic skins,' she says. 'Fish leather gives a more
elegant impression than traditional leather and it's
at least as strong.'

12 Making decisions

-*ing* forms

1 Complete this information leaflet about becoming a tour guide using the verbs from the box.

| interested in | can't help | enjoy | get used to | give up |
| imagine | look forward to | miss | resent | waste time |

Making decisions about your career?

Why not become a tour guide?

To be a tour guide, you have to be the sort of person who likes other people and you have to be an extrovert. Most tour guides, once they have been in the job for a year or two can't (1) .... having any other sort of job.

It's true that sometimes you have to get up really early to go to the airport to meet holidaymakers. But the only time you may (2) .... getting up early is when you get to the airport only to discover that the plane is two hours late!

Tour guides (3) .... seeing clients having a good time in the sun. When clients get to the resort most of them don't (4) .... unpacking – they head straight for the beach. They're not (5) .... hearing about additional tours they can do – not until the end of the first week, when they start getting a bit bored. As a tour guide, you (6) .... envying clients sometimes, when you know you've got to go to the office to catch up on work.

At the end of the season, most tour guides can (7) .... taking some time off and perhaps doing further training with a view to getting a promotion. However, although many tour guides want to get on in the company, this usually means working at head office and they may have to (8) .... working directly with the clients. They often (9) .... that client contact. On the other hand, tour guides soon (10) .... facing new challenges.

2 Some verbs can be followed by the *-ing* form or by the infinitive. Complete these sentences with the correct form of the verb in brackets.

1 The meeting was so interesting, we didn't even stop .... (have) a coffee break.
2 I'll never forget .... (take) the decision to start my own company. It's worked out really well.
3 Try .... (make) a list of all the advantages and disadvantages of going to that university.
4 Did you remember .... (complete) the questionnaire? You have to send it back before tomorrow.
5 I regret .... (turn down) that job. It would have been fun.

3 ⊙ The *Cambridge English Corpus* shows that advanced learners often make mistakes with prepositions and *-ing* forms. Correct the prepositions in bold in these sentences written by exam candidates.

1 This website is aimed **to** helping people find a job. ....
2 The course has been very useful **to** improving my business English. ....
3 If you are afraid **to** missing the train, arrive early at the station. ....
4 I am capable **to** translating all the necessary details. ....
5 You cancelled it **not** giving us a reasonable explanation. ....

4 Choose the correct option in these sentences written by exam candidates.

1 Everything you need is in the house, so there is no need *in getting / to get* confused.
2 Think twice before *printing / to print* this email.
3 I was really happy to hear about your decision *of spending / to spend* a few days in my country.
4 I am very happy *of hearing / to hear* from you.
5 Finally, I'd like to ask you *for considering / to consider* giving me a higher salary.
6 I would strongly recommend *using / to use* our booking system.
7 I suggest *booking / to book* better seats.
8 Don't worry about *writing / to write* to me if you have any questions.

Ⓖ → Student's Book page 168

Listening

1 🔊 **1 13** You will hear five short extracts in which people are talking about making decisions. While you listen, you must complete both tasks.

Task 1

Choose from the list (A–H) the difficulty each speaker had with making their decision.

A friends giving different advice
B having no previous experience of the situation   Speaker 1 ☐
C being under time pressure   Speaker 2 ☐
D not wanting to offend a relative   Speaker 3 ☐
E not wanting to appear weak   Speaker 4 ☐
F trying to please everyone   Speaker 5 ☐
G having conflicting feelings
H not having sufficient information

Task 2

Choose from the list (A–H) what happened to each speaker as a result of their decision.

A They embarked on a new career path.
B They invested in property.
C They got a promotion.   Speaker 1 ☐
D They became more self-confident.   Speaker 2 ☐
E They started a new hobby.   Speaker 3 ☐
F They felt more independent.   Speaker 4 ☐
G They became more relaxed.   Speaker 5 ☐
H They broke a promise.

Reading

1 You are going to read four extracts in which behavioural scientists discuss decision-making. For questions 1–5, choose from the behavioural scientists A–D. Each scientist may be chosen more than once.

Which behavioural scientist has a

1 different opinion from Hansford regarding the effects of bad decisions? ....

2 different view from Shibata about the influence of the power of suggestion? ....

3 different opinion to the others about whether personality plays a part in decision-making? ....

4 similar view to Latham on the influence of peer pressure in decision-making? ....

A Paul Latham

Interestingly, many business-training sessions which focus on helping managers make effective decisions fail to a large extent. It comes as no surprise to me to hear managers say things like 'in the end my decision was down to a sort of gut instinct'. So no matter what advice is given on courses, most people still resort to something intangible when it comes to making a decision. Understanding how we make decisions is important because it may help us to understand ourselves. If a person observes over time that they generally foresee a positive outcome from a decision, they may conclude that they are an optimist. However, this will rarely become the dominant factor influencing their decision-making, in the same way that the views of colleagues, for example, play only a small part.

B Angela Hansford

Without a doubt, the way people make decisions depends on their temperament rather than any external prompt. This can be observed both when people are making important decisions in their lives and when they are making relatively insignificant decisions. Those who decide against doing something more often than not fear an unsuccessful result whereas those with a positive outlook on life expect a favourable outcome. However, decision-making or rather the consequences of decisions is not as straightforward as that. Personally, I have observed that those who make a decision which has a negative outcome tend to go on to make further poor decisions. This may well be due to a decrease in their feeling of self-confidence. The next time they have to make a decision, the fear of an unsuccessful outcome is even greater.

C Dominik Panayotova

In my work, I have conducted research into how people make decisions. In particular, I have worked with politicians and educationalists. And as a result of my research, I believe that strong-minded people are able to make hard decisions and cautious people go to great lengths to weigh up all the pros and cons when consciously making a decision. However, when we look at the ordinary person in the street, if I can use that expression, I find that many of the small decisions that people make every day are made sub-consciously, and it goes without saying, these decisions are made intuitively. There has been no rational process before the decision has been made. And when you look at decision-making in general, these everyday decisions make up the bulk of the decisions that are made.

D Yoko Shibata

There have been several significant studies into the way people make decisions over the last decade. None of them, and rightly so in my view, concludes that decisions are made in a certain way as a result of an individual's character. The studies also show how little family and friends' opinions count in the decision-making process, and this is also borne out in my own research. Most studies include experiments in which people are for example, put into a cold and uncomfortable room and then asked to make a decision about something. As I would have predicted, in these circumstances, people become overly concerned about the unsuccessful outcome of their decisions. They are influenced by aspects of their surroundings. However, I am certain that most people who make a wrong decision actually learn from it and become better decision makers in the future as a result.

Reading and Use of English

1 For questions 1–8, read the text below and think of the word that best fits each gap. Use only one word for each gap.

Using colour in art

In the 20th century, Henri Matisse was part of a group of artists (0) __who__ enjoyed painting pictures with outrageously bold colours. The group were nicknamed 'Les Fauves'
(1) .... means 'wild beasts' in French. In Matisse's painting, 'The Open Window, Collioure', intense colour is used. The window frames and flower pots have all
(2) .... painted in a blazing red. These are a bold complement to
(3) .... greens that appear in other parts of the painting.
(4) .... order to arrange the various colours into an effective composition, the colour of the wall on the left is reflected in the right-hand window.

The apparent freedom of his style seems to suggest little skill, (5) .... when you begin to analyse his effective use of visual elements you realise that there is an instinctive talent at work. The key
(6) .... his success in using such colours was the realisation that he
(7) .... to simplify his drawing. He understood that (8) .... he intensified the colour for expressive effect, he must reduce the amount of detail he used.

Vocabulary

1 Replace the underlined adjectives in each sentence with a more evocative adjective from the box.

> deafening excruciating exquisite hilarious
> famished furious spotless terrified vibrant

1 He was obviously <u>afraid</u> at the thought of telling his tutor that he had ruined the painting by using the wrong colour. ....
2 The potter took out her creation from the kiln. When she finished the vase, she knew it would be <u>good</u> – the best thing she had ever made.

....
3 After spending the whole weekend redecorating my flat, my arm really hurts. In fact, any movement is <u>bad</u>. ....
4 Henry tells some <u>funny</u> stories about things that have happened to him. ....
5 The sky was full of threatening black clouds and the thunder was <u>loud</u>. ....
6 We were <u>hungry</u> so we ate the fruit even though its colour suggested it wasn't ripe. ....
7 She was <u>angry</u> because I'd bought yellow paint for the bedroom without consulting her.

....
8 The <u>nice</u> colours in the painting appealed to me instantly. ....
9 The kitchen was <u>clean</u> and the blue and white tiles were a perfect match with the colours in the blind. ....

Past tenses and the present perfect

1 **Complete the sentences with an appropriate form of the verbs in brackets. There is sometimes more than one possible answer.**

1 As the dark clouds .... (float) across the sky, I .... (realise) for the first time what it .... (feel) like to be truly alone.

2 Ever since she .... (live) in the cottage she .... (had) a wonderful feeling of being where she belonged.

3 When they .... (finish) their surveys, the students .... (start) to type up their findings.

4 As we .... (never do) research like this before, it .... (be) difficult to know how best to proceed.

5 It .... (be) the first time I .... (paint) in the open air and it was fantastic.

6 At the end of the day, we .... (be) exhausted as we .... (decorate) the kitchen for hours.

7 I couldn't remember when I .... (see) him before but his face .... (seem) familiar.

8 When .... (you last hear) from Dr Jones?

9 Is this the first time you .... (visit) Rome?

10 The photos .... (upload) yet.

11 I .... (not see) Jane for ages and then I .... (bump) into her twice last week.

12 He .... (follow) the path for at least half an hour before he sensed he .... (go) in the wrong direction.

13 I'm starving. I .... (not have) anything to eat since dinner last night.

14 I .... (drive) to work, Inspector, when the robbery .... (take) place.

15 Things .... (be) so much better since we .... (move) to a larger house.

16 .... (anybody see) my keys anywhere?

17 I .... (read) a ghost story when the storm .... (begin).

18 The mist .... (lift) just as we .... (reach) the peak.

19 The house was deserted; nothing .... (repair) for years and the roof .... (fall) in.

20 We .... (live) a lie for so many years, it .... (be) almost impossible to act like a normal couple again.

2 🔘 **The *Cambridge English Corpus* shows that advanced learners often make mistakes with the present perfect or the past simple. Choose the correct option in these sentences written by exam candidates.**

1 He *became / has become* rather stubborn and difficult to deal with when he got older.

2 We have polluted the air and water to such an extent that life *became / has become* less healthy.

3 The diet of young children *becomes / has become* worse and unbalanced.

4 Our modern way of working *has changed / changed* our habit of eating together with the whole family.

5 My speaking skills *are improved / have improved* a lot thanks to your special courses.

6 Mobile phones and technology in general *increased / have increased* the gaps between today's families.

7 I *have been / am* roller-blading since I was ten.

8 Who *had / has never* arrived home after an exhausting journey, sat down and said 'home sweet home'?

9 At the end, he *has been / was given* a questionnaire to complete.

10 All of us *has been / were* delighted.

3 **Advanced learners also often make mistakes with the present continuous and the present perfect continuous. Correct these sentences.**

1 For five years Kathy, is learning English at a private language school.

....

2 Lately, the business is looking up.

....

3 I know that she is dreaming about Australia for over 10 years.

....

4 This show is on our screens every day of the week since 2010.

....

5 For some years, a revolution is taking place regarding the role women play in society.

....

G → Student's Book page 169

Reading and Use of English

1 For questions 1–6, complete the second sentence so that it has a similar meaning to the first sentence, using the word given. You must use between three and six words, including the word given.

1 Jasmine started her course in Fine Art two years ago.
BEEN
Jasmine ....
Fine Art for two years.

2 The colour chart didn't make sense to me until Mike explained it.
HAD
Only when Mike ....
....
it make sense to me.

3 Even though we'd redecorated the sitting room, it still didn't seem very cosy.
DESPITE
Our siting room still didn't seem very cosy ....
.... it.

4 Lee loved her art being admired by experts in the field.
WHEN
Lee loved ....
....
by experts in the field.

5 The colour of the library walls will be changed as long as the college authorities agree to pay for it.
SUBJECT
The colour of the library walls will be changed ....
....
to pay for it.

6 There are fewer job opportunities for interior designers than there were ten years ago.
DECLINED
The number of job opportunities for interior designers ....
....
ten years.

2 For questions 1–8, read the text below. Use the word given in capitals at the end of some of the lines to form a word that fits the gap in the same line.

The importance of natural light in the workplace

Recent studies have confirmed the views expressed by workers for years.
(0) _Researchers_ have been monitoring workers in different offices. Employees working under artificial lights showed some (1)........................ characteristics. First, having no natural daylight resulted in workers having problems with (2)........................ Most were unable to work effectively for more than 20 minutes. Second, there were more instances of workers being (3)........................ or aggressive towards colleagues. This may lead to a breakdown in (4)........................ between co-workers.
(5)........................, cases such as these were not isolated and it is clear that relationships were being harmed. Third, workers reported an (6)........................ to get to sleep at night. Moreover, on average, they slept for 46 minutes less than workers who enjoyed natural light. In (7)........................, there is no doubt that working in a windowless office has serious affects. Employees' (8)........................ suffers, as does their general health.

RESEARCH

REMARK

CONCENTRATE

POLITE

FRIEND
FORTUNE

ABLE

CONCLUDE

PERFORM

Writing

1 Do the writing task below. Write your answer in 220–260 words.

You have attended a discussion on the effects of the lack of natural light on people in the workplace. You made the notes below.

Effects of lack of natural light:
- poor performance
- lack of co-operation
- deteriorating health

Some opinions expressed in the discussion:
'I can't believe that artificial lighting can lead to bad relationships between workers.'
'Inadequate lighting can lead to people experiencing headaches and other physical problems.'
'When sunlight falls on a screen, it's difficult to read the text.'

Write an **essay** for your tutor discussing **two of the effects** in your notes. You should explain **which effect is more serious** and provide reasons to support your opinion.

Vocabulary

1 Match words and phrases a–g using *talk* to their definitions 1–7.

a I'm not good at making small talk, especially at parties.

b She's very talkative, so I don't think there will be any awkward silences.

c She can talk the hind legs off a donkey.

d They're at a party. Why do they have to talk shop!

e Did you hear what happened to Anna yesterday? Oh, talk of the devil, here she is.

f The new statue in the park is the talk of the town.

g Today's talking point is: are women treated unfairly in the workplace?

1 talk a lot (but not too much)
2 talk about work
3 talk about unimportant things, usually to people you don't know well
4 talk too much
5 something which encourages discussion
6 said when a person appears, just after being talked about
7 what everyone is talking about

2 Complete these phrasal verbs with *talk* with words from the box.

out round down into over

1 I wish politicians wouldn't talk .... to us as if we were idiots.

2 After a very long conversation, he managed to talk me .... of leaving my job.

3 It's a good idea, but I'd like to talk it .... with my wife first.

4 She's not keen on the idea but we think we can talk her ....

5 I think I can talk him .... picking us up from the station.

3 Look again at the phrasal verbs in exercise 2 and answer these questions.

1 Which phrasal verbs mean *to persuade someone*?
.... , ... ,
....

2 Which means *to discuss something*?
....

3 Which means *to talk to someone as if they are stupid*? ....

The passive

1 Complete this text about how to give a good lecture with the correct form of the verbs in brackets.

The following tips **(1)** .... (adapt) from a book called *100 Tips for Lecturers*. They **(2)** .... (aim) at people who have little or no experience of lecturing. It is the responsibility of all lecturers to ensure that no student **(3)** .... (disadvantage) because of the poor quality of the lecturer's performance. A great deal **(4)** .... (write) on this subject. However, the essentials can **(5)** .... (summarise) as follows.

The first point of course is: know your subject. Make sure all possible research **(6)** .... (do).

Secondly, prepare your lecture thoroughly. Badly structured lectures are difficult to follow. Any handouts should **(7)** .... (write) clearly. Make sure there are enough copies.

Thirdly, think about your style of presentation. A lecture can **(8)** .... (ruin) by the lecturer standing in front of the screen so nothing can **(9)** .... (read). It may sound obvious, but it is easy to forget these things when you are concentrating on so many things at once.

Finally, make sure the audience **(10)** .... (give) tasks to do or questions to answer, so that they do not get bored.

2 Complete these sentences using an appropriate form of *have/get* + object / object pronoun + a verb from the box.

| ~~look at~~ check copy cut dry clean enlarge test redecorate |

1 My car's making a terrible noise. I'll *have to get it looked at* ....

2 I can't read small print any more. I ....
....

3 This photo is so good I ....
....

4 Our kitchen was looking really tatty and old-fashioned, so we ....
....

5 We can't copy the document here because our photocopier has broken down, so the secretary ....
somewhere else.

6 I think gas is leaking from your cooker – you should ....
....

7 The trouble is I can't wash this dress – I ....
....

8 My hairdresser is open today, so I'm going to ....
....
....

3 🎯 The *Cambridge English Corpus* shows that advanced learners often make mistakes with the passive. Correct these sentences written by exam candidates.

1 I can promise you that nobody is harmed so far by a member of the medical service.
....

2 I been invited to take part again as interpreter.
....

3 This new satellite TV series is being shown in our country for the last couple of weeks.
....

4 Along a path, which has be built for visitors, you will get to a row of farmers' houses.
....

5 Some of the classes on your course could be prepared better.
....

6 For example, this book is written with children in mind.
....

G → Student's Book page 170

Listening

1 **1 14** You will hear three different extracts. For questions 1–6, choose the correct answer (A, B or C) which fits best according to what you hear. There are two questions for each extract.

Extract 1

You overhear two people talking about changes in language.

1 What has the man just done?
   A completed a journalism course
   B written a language guide
   C found several grammatical errors in a book

2 How does the woman feel about the increased use of lower-case letters?
   A It is not a trend that she believes will last.
   B It makes text look unattractive and complex.
   C It can lead to misunderstandings when she reads.

Extract 2

You overhear two students discussing language learning.

3 What do they both enjoy about the approach their Russian teacher uses?
   A She encourages students to access a range of material on the internet.
   B She does not criticise students for making mistakes in class.
   C She acknowledges that students' learning styles are different

4 The girl was initially attracted to learning Russian because
   A she wanted to read Russian literature in the original language.
   B she intends to take advantage of business opportunities in Russia.
   C she hopes to travel extensively in Russia in the near future.

Extract 3

You overhear two students discussing a lecture on how humans produce language.

5 The woman hadn't realised that human mouth is suited to producing sounds because
   A the lips have a complex system of muscles.
   B the tongue is short and flat.
   C the teeth are different sizes.

6 What information does the man say he had read about before?
   A Humans can develop speech at an early age.
   B Humans can swallow and breathe at the same time.
   C Humans can alter their breathing rhythm when speaking.

Writing

1 **Do the writing task below.**

You see this notice on a website that you frequently visit.

> The Language Society would like to encourage a wider range of people to learn languages. The Director of the Society invites you to send a proposal outlining the possible reasons for some people not learning languages and explaining what can be done to overcome these difficulties. A decision will then be made as to how the Language Society can best promote language learning.

Write your proposal in 220–260 words in an appropriate style.

In my view ...

Reading

1 Read this article about the effects of low light on people in the far north. Choose from the paragraphs (A–G) the one that fits each gap (1–6). There is one extra paragraph which you do not need to use.

EXPRESSING YOURSELF IN A COLD CLIMATE

Bidge Hanson and his neighbours, in the world's most northerly university town, spent yesterday pretty much in the dark, again. In Tromsø, 200 miles north of the Arctic Circle, it was yet another day when the sun failed to put in an appearance. In winter, the Norwegian town and its 60,000 people live life in a permanent night, and in the summer they switch to spending months in perpetual daylight.

1

For more than a year, doctors tracked volunteers, measuring their cognitive performances in tests in both winter and summer, expecting the results to support the view that in winter people are prone to a range of negative symptoms, in addition to depression associated with seasonal affective disorder (SAD).

2

'We tested 1,000 people on a battery of cognitive tests, including memory, attention, recognition time, memory recall and confusability. We didn't look at depression, we were interested in cognitive performance. We tested them in summer and in winter, and we were sure that we would be able to pick up the winter deficit that is so often talked about.'

3

Even on the simplest of the tests, the winter performances were better. The reaction times of the volunteers were, on average, 11 milliseconds quicker in the winter tests. The problem that Dr Brennen and his colleagues now have is explaining what kind of body mechanism could be at work to produce the unexpected phenomenon of superior thinking in winter. It is at odds with many assumptions about health and the winter. A National Institute of Mental Health survey of 1,500 SAD patients in the US found that 90% reported decreased activity in winter. They also reported lack of energy and an increased need for sleep.

4

Some suspect that a change in the environment, especially the arrival of long dark nights, affects personality – that when it gets cold and dark, man becomes more introverted and more focused on the task in hand.

5

'One possible explanation is that we are less distracted by other things in winter. There is not so much to look at and therefore a greater opportunity for you to attend to your tasks,' she says.

6

But just how light works is not clear. 'Although the cause of SAD is not known, research so far suggests that it is triggered by a seasonal disruption in the cycling of the hormone melatonin, which throws the circadian rhythms off balance,' says Professor William Regelson of Virginia University.

A

'It is a quite surprising and counter-intuitive finding that requires a lot of thought,' says Professor Anne Farmer of the Institute of Psychiatry in London, who specialises in treating affective disorders, including SAD.

B

'If you read a lot of the literature on SAD, the psychiatrists expect concentration to be worse in winter, that memory will be poor, and that people will feel sluggish. But we found no trace of that. Clearly the belief that people get more forgetful in the winter months is unfounded. The findings contradict some of the claims found in the literature on SAD.'

C

And they may be implicated in the mechanism behind the Tromsø results for cognitive performance, because a similar finding of depression and improved or unaffected mental performance is found in one other body cycle.

D

For psychologists, the extremes in this Arctic Circle environment made it the perfect place to study the effects of the seasons on the mind, and to investigate whether there is any foundation for long-held views that in winter, performance slows down. If the theory was right, any effect would, they figured, be magnified at a latitude of 69 degrees north.

E

For the treatment of the depression associated with SAD, Professor Farmer and an increasing number of doctors are advising using light boxes. It's been found that exposure to bright artificial light can reduce the symptoms of depression by as much as 80% in some patients. Research on people with SAD has also found that their symptoms improve the nearer they live to the equator.

F

SAD, which affects between 1% and 25% of people, is accepted as a condition where depression is linked to winter. But depression and improved cognitive performance are strange bedfellows, so the hunt is on to find out what could be happening in the brain to produce such a paradox. Investigators are looking at whether light or temperature may be at work.

G

But when measured by cognitive performance, it was found that the people of Tromsø were brighter and quicker in the winter months, a result that put a large spanner in the works of those that hold that people are slower in the winter. For Dr Tim Brennen, who led the research, the results were a big surprise.

Vocabulary

1 **Match these expressions from the article with their definitions.**

1 prone to
2 to put a spanner in the works
3 at odds with
4 strange bedfellows
5 the task in hand

a very different from
b very different people who are connected in a way you would not expect
c likely to suffer from (an illness) or having a tendency towards (something bad)
d the job which is important at the present moment
e to upset people's activities or plans

2 **Now match these adjectives from the article with their definitions.**

1 dull
2 sluggish
3 groggy
4 unfounded
5 counter-intuitive

a acting more slowly and with less energy or power than usual
b not based on fact; untrue
c something does not happen in the way you expect it to
d not very intelligent or interesting
e weak and unable to think clearly or walk correctly, usually because of tiredness or illness

3 **Match these nouns from the article with their definitions.**

1 findings
2 battery
3 trace
4 fatigue
5 trigger

a a sign that something has happened or existed
b something which causes (something bad) to happen
c large number of things of a similar type
d official discovery
e tiredness

The infinitive

1 **Complete these sentences with an appropriate form of the verbs from the box. Sometimes there may be more than one possible answer.**

afford arrange fail intend invite manage
pretend suppose tend want gain

1 The police officer .... to notice the scrap of paper tucked in the back of the diary.
2 In order .... entry to the house, the man .... to be conducting a survey for the government.
3 Cats .... to be more independent than dogs.
4 I .... to look for a new job once I've finished my training here.
5 We .... to pull the child to safety from the river.
6 I .... to see that new film that's on in town – it's .... to be really good.
7 We .... to meet at 4 o'clock, so I don't know why he isn't here.
8 We can't .... to go on holiday this year, so we'll .... some friends to come and stay with us.

2 **Complete the sentences with the correct form of the verbs in brackets. More than one correct answer may be possible.**

1 It's nice .... (sit) here with you.
2 I meant .... (phone) you earlier but it completely slipped my mind.
3 I would have liked .... (take part) in the debate on television. It would have given me great pleasure .... (sit) there when he said we could have more funding.
4 There is a wide range of topics .... (cover) in this term's programme.
5 She ought .... (ask) her opinion at least, before we decide.
6 Try .... (not be) too nervous at the interview.
7 I would rather .... (invite) Maria than Paula.
8 He made us .... (work) until 8 o'clock.

9 She lets her children .... (watch) whatever they like on TV.
10 .... (include) Sarah would have been a big mistake.
11 Why .... (go) to the library when you can look it up on the internet?
12 All I did was .... (ask) if she was all right!
13 .... (retire) at 30 would be perfect.
14 For him .... (win) the match would be a dream come true.
15 Would it be easier for me .... (talk) to you about it later?
16 The plan is for us .... (take) the tents and to sleep in the forest.
17 I need you .... (help) me.
18 There's nothing for the children .... (eat).
19 There isn't enough time .... (explain) everything now.
20 It's important for there .... (be) plenty of time left for discussion at the end of the talk.

3 ◉ **The *Cambridge English Corpus* shows that advanced learners often make mistakes with the infinitive. Choose the correct option in these sentences, written by exam candidates.**

1 I recommend *getting / to get* further information.
2 In addition, I had the opportunity *to meet / meet* very interesting people.
3 I suggest *to interview / interviewing* Mr Brown.
4 I don't have any difficulty *managing / to manage* a basic conversation in those languages.
5 If you have any problems *to get / getting* to my place, just give me a ring.
6 If I had the chance *of live / to live* in Istanbul, then I would.
7 You have little chance *of winning / to win* the lottery.

G → Student's Book page 171

16 Who we are

Inversion

1 Rewrite these sentences to be emphatic, starting with the words given. They all involve inversion.

1 We are in no way responsible for what happened.
In no way ....
....

2 He puts in an appearance himself only on very rare occasions.
Only on very rare occasions
....
....

3 You shouldn't on any account just do what they say without thinking it through yourself.
On no account ....
....

4 John had no sooner sold his house than the one he was hoping to buy fell through.
No sooner ....
....

5 I little imagined that I would ever meet a famous Hollywood film star.
Little ....
....

6 You mustn't at any time let anyone know what you are really doing here.
At no time ....
....

7 I've never stayed in a such a bad hotel before.
Never ....
....

2 ⦿ The *Cambridge English Corpus* shows that advanced learners often make mistakes with inversion and word order. Correct these sentences, written by exam candidates.

1 Not only the food was dull, but also the service was not what you stated in the brochure.
....

2 I would be pleased to try this job for one week. Only then I will be sure if I like it.
....

3 Not only it was wrong, but there were not enough minibuses to transport us.
....

4 Not only there was no choice for vegetarians, but also the food was inedible.
....

5 Some food companies believe that only in this way people can be interested in buying their product.
....

6 Perhaps could we do the test again?
....

7 Your hotel was not cheap. Nor I can accept that you offer high standards of service or food.
....

8 If I could choose any time or place, then definitely would I choose the US in the 1960s.
....

9 Anyway, you asked me what should you wear.
....

10 Not until you have passed your driving test you should drive a car alone.
....

3 Complete these sentences with your own words. They should all use inversion.

1 Seldom ....
....

2 Not until ....
....

3 Little ....
....

4 Under no circumstances ....
....

5 Only ....
....

Ⓖ → Student's Book page 171

Vocabulary

1 **Complete each set of idioms (1–8) with a part of the body. Each set matches with one of the body parts illustrated on this page.**

1 a be on the tip of your ....
  b bite your ....
  c say something ....in-cheek
2 a bite someone's .... off
  b keep your .... above water
  c bang your .... against a brick wall
3 a put your .... down
  b put your .... in it
  c not put a .... wrong
4 a break someone's ....
  b do something to your ....'s content
  c feel your .... sink
5 a turn a deaf ....
  b play something by ....
  c keep your .... to the ground
6 a keep your .... to the grindstone
  b pay through the ....
  c turn your .... up at something
7 a catch someone's ....
  b see .... to ....
  c cast your .... over something
8 a keep your .... in something
  b give someone a ....
  c get out of ....

2 **Now match the idioms from exercise 1 with the definitions below.**

1 not quite be able to remember something ..1a..
2 be ironic ....
3 speak to someone angrily ....
4 tell someone firmly that they must do something ....
5 behave perfectly ....
6 decide how to deal with a situation as it develops ....
7 make someone very unhappy ....
8 do something as much as you want to ....
9 feel despairing ....
10 get out of control ....
11 pretend not to hear ....
12 have a quick look at something ....
13 have just enough money to live on ....
14 have the same opinion ....
15 continue working very hard without stopping ....
16 be noticed by someone ....
17 practise a skill so that you do not lose it ....
18 help someone ....
19 keep trying to achieve or communicate something, but with no success ....
20 keep silent ....
21 reject something because you don't feel it's good enough for you ....
22 say something tactless ....
23 spend far too much on something ....
24 watch and listen carefully to what is happening around you ....

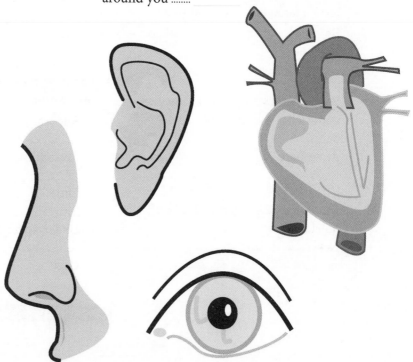

Reading and Use of English

1 Complete the following article by writing the missing words in the gaps. Use only one word for each gap.

Our amazing bodies

The human body is remarkable **(0)** ......*in*...... many different ways. **(1)** .... we all have one, few of us are aware of many remarkable facts about what exactly it consists **(2)** .... Few people realise, for example, that human bones are four times stronger than concrete. Or that most of the cells in the body renew **(3)** .... every two or three weeks. Or that the surface area of a human lung is equal to **(4)** .... of a tennis court. Or even that, in the course of just 24 hours, blood circulating round the body covers a total of 19,000 kilometres, **(5)** .... is the equivalent of going from the UK to New Zealand. These are just **(6)** .... of the many extraordinary facts about our human body.

Most of us take our bodies **(7)** .... granted. Yet, really, we should give them a great deal of respect. **(8)** .... it not for their amazing powers, we would not be able to live the lives we do.

Listening

1 🔊 **15** Listen to the start of a lecture entitled 'Sense and Sensitivity'. Choose the best answer (A, B, C or D) according to the lecture.

1 The lecturer explains that the 'hidden body senses' are important because
   A they alert us to potentially dangerous situations.
   B our bodies would become poisoned without them.
   C our bodies work to their full potential, thanks to them.
   D they only detect changes within our bodies.

2 In this part of the lecture she is aiming to
   A explain the limitations of the five senses.
   B describe the complexity of the body.
   C highlight the importance of the heart.
   D recommend a particular book.

2 **How accurately did you listen? Complete these sentences, then listen again to check.**

1 Cells can .... the temperature within and outside our bodies.
2 The heart must pump blood around the body to .... essential oxygen and nutrients to all the cells and tissues in the body.
3 The heart can .... to training, stress and long-term needs.
4 Millions of pieces of information from .... throughout the body are relayed, ... and integrated, often within the brain.
5 The next task is .... the appropriate responses – sometimes in less than a second.

Reading

1 Look at the photos, which accompany four magazine reviews, and think about what the four reviews might be about.

2 Read these reviews and answer these questions for each.

1 What is being reviewed?
2 Which words and phrases helped you to determine what was being reviewed?
3 Which words or phrases serve to convey opinion as opposed to facts?

A

The combination of a long wheelbase and a high roofline creates plenty of space inside the Picasso. Its gear stick is mounted on the dashboard, not between the Picasso's two front seats, leaving a large amount of wasted space on the floor. The centre rear seat folds to make a table between the other two. Much creative thinking has gone into this table so that it can double as a desktop for work purposes (complete with document clip to stop papers sliding around) and as a picnic table with cupholders. Equal ingenuity has been applied to finding space for the 30 pockets and compartments that are dotted around the Picasso's cabin. Some are better than others. The pocket under the dashboard on the driver's side is too shallow to hold a mobile phone securely and if a pocket won't even hold a mobile, what's the use of it?

1 ....
2 ....
3 ....

B

So one of my dining companions discovered to her cost that mistakes are possible, even with the more conventional dishes on the menu. Yet another found that there is even more potential for disaster if you follow their suggestion of mixing and matching. In theory (strange but true!) you can mingle roast duckling with a sweet pineapple and vanilla sauce. One of us decided not to leave it as theory, but to try it out in practice. The duck was adequate, the sauce turned out to be sickly sweet.

1 ....
2 ....
3 ....

C

This is a chocolate box of a movie: sweet and gooey and enjoyably bad for you. It transports the always watchable James Lowe to a seaside setting, where he meets the beautiful daughter of a kind boat owner. You can probably join the dots from there. It's silly, but beautifully executed silliness, and a haven for those seeking refuge from the pressures of work.

1 ....
2 ....
3 ....

When you listen to the first tracks, there is nothing that makes you think this is special, but then there is a big change. Suddenly, the man who wrote one of the great songs about unrequited love, 'I Can't Forget You', is back ... telling us how it is. Just because you are rich and appear to be massively successful, it doesn't mean you don't feel down and out and bitterly disappointed with the world on occasion.

1 ....
2 ....
3 ....

2 **In the reviews, what collocates with each of these words?**

1 for work ....
2 strange but ....
3 sickly ....
4 join ....
5 seek ....
6 unrequited ....
7 bitterly ....

Writing

1 Do the writing task below. Write your review in 220–260 words.

> A website has asked readers for reviews of a book that relates to their own lives in some way. Reviews should explain how the book relates to the reviewer's life and should also comments on the book's strengths and weaknesses.

Reading and Use of English

1 Complete the second sentence so it has a similar meaning to the first sentence, using the word given. Do not change the word given. You must use between three and six words, including the word given.

1 People say that eating a large meal just before bedtime means you sleep less well.
SUPPOSED
Eating a large meal just before bedtime .... a negative effect on how well you sleep.

2 I thought I must be imagining things when I saw Dan on the doorstep.
EYES
I .... when I saw Dan on the doorstep.

3 Perhaps Fiona forgot to take her newspaper with her when she got off the train.
MAY
Fiona .... the train when she got off.

4 It's a pity we paid so much to have the car repaired.
SPENT
I wish .... getting the car repaired.

5 The author couldn't think what to call his novel.
COME
The author wasn't able .... for his novel.

6 It doesn't bother Norma if everyone is looking at her.
CENTRE
Norma doesn't .... attention.

Articles

1 Add articles *a, an* or *the* to each sentence.

1 Information you find on internet is not always reliable.
2 Her boyfriend is solicitor.
3 He is solicitor you were reading about in newspaper week ago.
4 I earn about £8,000 year from setting and marking exams.
5 Smith family have gardener who comes in from time to time, who they pay by hour.
6 We should have dinner together at Holiday Inn in New Square some time in next few weeks.
7 We spent week on holiday in Seychelles but I spent most of week in bed as I caught nasty cold.
8 Family are all in different places this week – Joan has gone to US and Monty is in India, while Sue has gone by car to north of Scotland and Bob has taken train to France.

2 Complete these sentences with the correct form of phrases from the box. They all contain singular nouns used without an article.

> by word of mouth   to be lying face down
> to be out of pocket   to catch fire
> to make way for   to set sail   to sigh with relief
> to talk sense

1 Paul is rather impractical with some of his suggestions but Maria always
   ....
2 We'll pay you back for what you bought for the picnic. We don't want you ....
3 Emma .... when she saw the children getting safely off the plane.
4 The ship .... at midday tomorrow. Let's go down to wave it off.
5 The man .... by the side of the road. I presumed he had been knocked off his bike.
6 They suspect that the trees .... because someone failed to put a cigarette out properly.
7 The best way to get business is
   ....
8 Please .... the food trolley.

3 Complete these sentences in any way appropriate.

1 The older you get, ...
2 ...., the less I liked him.
3 The sooner you make up your minds,
   ....
4 ...., the happier I am.
5 The more energy you put into something,
   ....

4 Rewrite these sentences using the words in brackets so that they have the same meaning.

1 I'm afraid I don't have much money. (only; little)
   ....
2 I've got about half a dozen euros. (few)
   ....
3 All the girls in the class have their own email address. (each)
   ....
4 Not many people pass their driving test the first time. (few)
   ....
5 He doesn't have much experience of hard manual work. (little)
   ....

5 ⊙ The *Cambridge English Corpus* shows that advanced learners often make mistakes with articles. Correct these sentences.

1 You may have to queue for couple of hours.
   ....
2 I have been in London for few years.
   ....
3 We have a plenty of different programmes on TV.
   ....
4 We are having an athletics competition the next month.
   ....
5 We believe that opening the centre to public would be a good solution.
   ....
6 The speech was cancelled at last minute.
   ....
7 I'm sure she will invite you to have the breakfast with her.
   ....
8 We should use the public transport more often and not depend on cars.
   ....

G→ Student's Book page 172

Telling the truth

Le Moulin de la Galette (Pierre August Renoir, Paris 1876)

Listening

1 **1 16 Listen to two people talking about a painting.**

1 What does the young man say that the painting shows?
A British life in the early 20th century
B late 19th-century café society
C how rich people used to entertain themselves
D the contrasts between rich and poor

2 What does the young man say characterises the artist's style?
A his precision
B his colour contrasts
C his impressionistic approach
D his use of light and shade

3 How does the woman feel about the young man?
A impressed by his originality
B interested in his attention to detail
C amused by his attempts to impress her
D surprised by his lack of knowledge

4 What does the woman say is unusual about the painting?
A its impressionistic use of light and colour
B its depiction of people from ordinary backgrounds
C its choice of subject-matter for a painting of this size
D its affectionate portrayal of a Parisian café

Emphasis

1 **Rewrite these sentences.**

1 I find it hard making small talk when I meet someone new.
What I ....
....

2 Parents usually enjoy talking about their children.
What parents ....
....

3 You can be thought of as a good conversationalist if you just ask someone about themselves and then sit back and listen to the answer.
All you need to do ....
....

4 When you're making small talk, it's probably better not to talk about very serious topics.
The sensible thing to do ....
....

5 She is very good at making small talk.
What immediately struck me ....
....

G → Student's Book page 172

Reading

1 Choose which of the paragraphs (A–G) fit into the gaps (1–6).
There is one extra paragraph which you do not need to use.

Small talk at the First Tuesday Club

In retrospect, wearing the red sticker was a mistake. As a journalist, I technically had no right to it – red stickers were supposed to be for bankers – but, once I'd put it on, people seemed to want to talk to me. They came in pairs. Keen young business people with the next Big Idea. Online petfood? Two-hour shirt delivery? They pinned me to the wall, slipped their business cards into my pocket and pushed business plans into my hand. With a red sticker, I was their man, their ticket to a fortune, and all they needed was a quick hit. Say 10 million or so.

1 [_____]

A matchmaking club of more than 40,000 members, First Tuesday takes wannabe entrepreneurs and, with a little luck and hard work, aims to make them millionaires. Upon arrival, entrepreneurs are given green stickers, the bankers with funds to hand out red stickers and everyone else – lawyers, salesmen, consultants and journalists – yellow stickers.

2 [_____]

The fashion for meetings like these grew from the spirit of entrepreneurism that blossomed around the Internet in the late 1990s. The computer network that for 30 years had been the exclusive club of a few physicists suddenly became available to the rest of us when a young Englishman named Tim Berners-Lee invented a way to share documents and pictures between users. In a move never properly acknowledged, Berners-Lee did something special: he gave the technology away for free and the World Wide Web was born.

3 [_____]

The theory is enticing: anyone with anything to sell, from carpet weavers in Peru to English steelworks, can reach the whole world with just a simple website. Outsource – in other words, get someone else to worry about – your delivery problems and a multi-million pound business can be run from your bedroom.

4 [_____]

Indeed, size would be a disadvantage in the new economy. Why incur the cost of building a network of stores when a website, a warehouse and a way to deliver are sufficient? The problem was that anyone with an interest in the internet was unlikely to know anything about venture capital and, even if they did, the venture capitalists were not interested in technobabble-speaking geeks.

5 [_____]

So, in October ten years or so ago, some entrepreneurs held a party. They realised that putting people with ideas in the same room as people with money, shutting the doors could be the recipe for something special. It was an instant success. The casual atmosphere took away the pressure from both sides and now anyone with an idea, no matter how crazy, could meet as many bankers as they could handle in an evening. Within months, First Tuesday events were appearing everywhere. Now First Tuesday is the traditional rite of passage for anyone with an internet idea. The pioneers of the first meeting are long since up and running: today's attendees are the rest of us.

6 [_____]

Then the lucky ones will be emailed back with details of the next get-together and their invite to untold riches.

A Then, as now, the bankers didn't quite understand these people. They'd help them, but they didn't want them in the house. What was needed was neutral territory – somewhere for the two camps to meet, where neither would feel overwhelmed.

B Put them all in the same room, dim the lighting, add canapés and cocktails, and a few inspirational speeches to set the mood, then sit back and let nature take its course.

C The popularity of the evenings and the number of people with business plans is such that the green-stickered hopefuls forever outnumber the red-stickered bankers. Sticker hunting is the new blood sport and many red stickers try to hide their true identity.

D No need for expensive shops, no need for hundreds of employees, no need for middlemen to eat into your profits. With everyone's shopfront restricted to the size of the PC screen, there is no advantage in being a global giant.

E Anyone can apply – the student with his loan cheque for capital; the pensioner with a clever idea; the mad, the bad and the just plain hopeful – all they have to do is log on to First Tuesday's website, register their interest and wait.

F She was a precocious child. From a handful of particle physics notes in December 1990, the Web grew to more than a billion pages in less than a decade. As with all things human, it wasn't long before people began to see that the Web offered more than a vast global library: maybe you could make money too. E-commerce was about to begin.

G It was the first Tuesday of last month when, like every month, thousands of hopeful people converged, clutching business plans in sweat-stained folders, on venues in more than 50 cities around the world. They were there to get rich. They were there for First Tuesday.

Vocabulary

1 Here are some phrases from the article. Match the first parts of the phrases (1–12) with their endings (a–l).

1 are long since up
2 as many … as
3 don't want someone
4 it was a mistake
5 it wasn't long
6 let nature
7 take away
8 they pinned me
9 thousands of people
10 to eat
11 to reach
12 to set

a the whole world
b anyone could have made
c they can handle
d the pressure
e into your profits
f and running
g the mood
h in the house
i take its course
j against the wall
k before people began
l converged

2 Use a good learner's dictionary to find more chunks based on each of these words.

a nature ....
b let ....
c course ....
d set ....
e mood ....

Do it for my sake

Reading and Use of English

1 Read the text below and think of the word which best fits each gap. Use only one word in each gap.

Recent research (0) ....*into*........ how people influence others has provided some interesting case studies. For example, a recent study provides some effective examples, such as (1) .... of Lisa Robinson who was waiting to board a plane flying to Austria, when the flight was cancelled.

There were about a hundred of us stranded,' she says. '(2) .... else was yelling at the airport staff.

But I didn't join in. I walked up to the man behind the ticket desk very quietly and said, "This (3) .... be so awful for you!

I don't know (4) ....you deal with these situations. I could never handle it as well (5) .... you are." And so it happened that (6) .... my even asking, he found me a seat on another airline with an upgrade to first class. He was happy to do a favour for someone who was appreciative (7) .... of hostile.'

Flattery is an essential element of the sweet-talk strategy. 'It's human psychology that stroking a person's ego with a (8) .... well-directed compliments makes them want to prove you right,' explains the author of the book.

Listening

1 **1·17** Listen to a psychology tutor talking about some research which has been carried out into influencing people. Complete the notes.

The impact of flattery

The tutor says she immediately recognises when her **(1)** .... is insincerely praised.

She is reporting on a study which took place in **(2)** ....

She says that the study chose to focus on a sports centre because its clientele was generally quite **(3)** ....

The sports centre ad praised its readers for their **(4)** .... attitude towards keeping fit.

The study's ultimate aim was to discover whether the ads had an impact on subjects' **(5)** .... even when their tricks had been recognised.

She says that people tend to consider that they are better than **(6)** .... in their abilities and characteristics.

She gives the example of someone's **(7)** .... being praised as an example of flattery being unconsciously accepted as the truth.

She describes a supplementary experiment in which subjects had to write about an aspect of their own **(8)** .... that they were either happy or unhappy about.

2 Complete the word formation table based on words from the listening text.

Noun	Verb	Adjective
flattery, ...	....	....
....	instruct	....
....	....	straight
....	expect	....
....	....	desperate
....	apply	....
compliment	....	....

Writing

1 Do the writing task below.

> A television company is preparing a series of programmes about the lives of young people in different countries. It has asked viewers to send in proposals explaining why their country should be included in the series. The proposal should also describe what aspects of the lives of young people in your country should be considered and should include your suggestions for the format the programme should take.

Write a **proposal** in 220–260 words.

Reading and Use of English

1 Complete the second sentence so it has a similar meaning to the first, using the word given. Do not change the word given. You must use between three and five words, including the word given.

1 I'd like you to write me a report briefly portraying each member of the team.
BRIEF
I'd like you to write me a report which contains

....

each member of the team.

2 I want your report to investigate how each member of the team differs from the others.
GO
Your report should ....

....

the members of the team.

3 Please could you examine the values and beliefs influencing their working relationships?
HAVE
Please could you examine the values and beliefs

....

their working relationships.

4 The report should consider how teams can function differently.
WAYS
I'd like your report ....

....

which teams can function.

5 I'd like you to conclude your report by explaining why the team is currently behaving as it is.
REASON
Please conclude your report by ....

....

the team's current behaviour.

6 What I'm trying to say is that we should all work harder.
POINT
The ....

....

is that we should all work harder.

Language of persuasion

1 Read the dialogues below. Who do you think is speaking in each case? In other words, is the conversation more formal or more informal?

1 A: Couldn't you be persuaded to give it a try?
B: Well, if you were to show me once again, I suppose I might consider attempting it myself.

....

....

....

2 A: What would you recommend as our best course of action?
B: I would suggest that the most sensible approach might be to continue along the same lines as at present.

....

....

....

3 A: Where's the station?
B: I'll drop you off there on my way to work if you like.

....

....

....

4 A: Did you like the film?
B: No, it was awful!

....

....

....

5 A: Would you mind telling me what I should do next?
B: Certainly, sir. If you just complete this form, then you should hand it in at the desk over there.

....

....

....

2 Rewrite each dialogue in the opposite style (i.e. if it is formal, write it in a more informal style).

G → Student's Book page 173

We are what we eat

Listening

1 You are going to listen to a lecture about a survey. Here are some words which are often used when reporting on a survey. Match them to their meanings (1–11).

a indicate
b respondent
c claim
d mean
e frequency
f proportion
g prevalent
h majority
i cumulative
j contribute to
k be concerned with

1 part of a group compared to the whole
2 how often something occurs
3 be a factor in
4 suggest
5 larger part of something
6 increasing by one addition after another
7 person questioned in a survey
8 be interested in
9 state that something is true
10 happening very often
11 average

2 1 18 Listen to the sociology lecture and complete the notes. Write one or two words in each gap.

The sociology of eating out

Sociologists are interested in who eats out in different places and **(1)** .... they eat there.

The study under discussion
- asked people about their eating habits
- did not include either eating at work or **(2)** ....

Results
Typically, the subjects of the survey ate out once in **(3)** ....

Percentages of eating out
- once a week: **(4)** ....
- at least monthly: **(5)** ....
- never: **(6)** ....

Eating out at someone else's home
- percentage never eating at a family member's home: **(7)** ....
- proportion never eating at a friend's home: **(8)** ....

Conclusions
Eating out is seen by sociologists as part of the way in which people establish their **(9)** ....
They are interested in ways in which patterns of **(10)** .... help someone to demonstrate their status in society.
Using or not using particular **(11)** .... can be shown to be one way whereby people display their social class.

Vocabulary

1 Complete this table based on words from the lecture.

Noun	Verb	Adjective	Adverb
		different	differently
		financial	
			systematically
respondent			
	exclude		
		(in)frequent	
		prevalent	–
	attribute		–
refinement			–
superiority	–		–
distinction			

2 Complete these sentences with the correct form of words from the table.

1 There was a .... smell of cigarette smoke in my hotel room.
2 With modern computer technology, linguists have far more reliable information about .... than used to be possible.
3 Trees are dying in areas where acid rain is most ....
4 Some scholars have .... these poems to Francis Bacon rather than Shakespeare.
5 Her business idea seems very sound, but now she has to find someone to help her .... it.
6 This room is for the .... use of guests.
7 How many people .... to the job advert in the newspaper?
8 Engineers spent many months .... the software.
9 Unfortunately, Peter suffers from a bit of a .... complex.
10 What's the .... between these two types of software?
11 You're so disorganised – you really need a better .... of working.

Hypothesising

1 Complete the missing words in these sentences. The first letter is given.

1 Interviewers often like to present a h... case and ask interviewees how they would deal with such a situation.
2 Just i... if she was offered the job in Paris!
3 Let us a... that everyone applying for the job will speak fluent French.
4 W... they to offer her the position in the Rio branch, do you think she'd accept it?
5 On the a... that she would, do you think we'd be able to visit her there?
6 A... for the fact that she hasn't got all that much experience, I think she's very likely to be offered something.
7 P... it isn't necessary to have a driving licence, she's in with a good chance.
8 S... for a moment, I think that she might be asked at the interview for her views on the current political situation.
9 I w... whether Jane will get an interview for the job she's applied for.
10 Let us s... that she accepts the job – how would you then feel about her moving abroad?

2 Choose the correct words. Sometimes both answers may be possible.

1 I don't think you've accounted *from* / *for* the fact that July is a very busy time of the year.
2 Imagine *whether* / *if* I got accepted on the course. Wouldn't it be fantastic?
3 I wonder *whether* / *if* James is coming tonight.
4 Were he *to be* / *be* offered the job, I'm not sure he would accept.
5 Suppose I *offered* / *to offer* to lend you the money. What would you say?

3 Rewrite these sentences using the words in brackets. The sentences should retain the same meaning.

1 Providing she gets the questions she's prepared for, she should do very well in the exam. (long)

....

2 In your shoes, I'd resign on the spot. (you)

....

3 He's only agreed to help finance the project because he assumes that she is also going to put in an equal amount. (assumption)

....

4 Had we anticipated what problems might arise, we would never have embarked on such a complex venture. (if)

....

5 I wonder whether Laura still thinks about me. (love)

....

6 Suppose we make no changes at all for the time being? (what)

....

7 Let's imagine a situation where a single mother is bringing up two children. (case)

....

8 I wish I knew how she felt about things. (if)

....

9 Do you think that they will win the World Cup? (wonder)

....

10 What if I ask her out on a date and she says 'no'? (suppose)

....

G → Student's Book page 173

Writing

1 **Do the writing task below. Write 220–260 words in an appropriate style.**

Your class has listened to a radio discussion about ways of encouraging young people to eat more healthily. You have made the notes below.

Ways of encouraging young people to eat more healthily:

- school lessons
- TV programmes
- working with parents

Some opinions expressed in the discussion:

'Teachers can explain why eating healthily is important.'
'Popular TV stars can have a strong influence on how children behave.'
'How young people eat is their parents' responsibility.'

Write an **essay** for your tutor, discussing **two** of the ways in your notes. You should explain which is the more effective way of encouraging young people to eat more healthily and provide reasons to support your opinion.

You may, if you wish, make use of the opinions expressed in the discussion, but you should use your own words as far as possible.

Natural wonders

Listening

1 Look at photos 1–3 on this page. Which information do you think matches each photo?

    a long ocean bay ....
    b 9.4 kilometres in circumference ....
    c tidal power ....
    d stretches over 12,000 square kilometres ....
    e east coast ....
    f 318 metres high ....
    g steeped in history ....
    h spiritual significance ....
    i smoking volcano ....
    j plateau ....
    k geysers ....
    l a habitat for 12 species of whale ....
    m vibrant in colour ....
    n steep climb ....
    o salt lake ....

2 **1 19** Listen to three people describing a place they would like to nominate as one of the 'Seven Wonders of Nature'. Check your answers to exercise 1.

3 Listen again. Match statements a–g to the people in the recording (1–3).

    a uses a lot of descriptive language ....
    b mentions something that will attract lovers of fine dining ....
    c gives information about the elimination process in the campaign to become one of the 'Seven Wonders of Nature' ....
    d recommends visiting the place in order to appreciate it fully ....
    e mentions the alternative energy benefits of the place ....
    f describes something that is poisonous to wildlife ....
    g describes a place that has an alternative name ....

Range of grammatical structures

1 You are going to read an article about a young person who wants to conquer Mount Everest. Read the first two paragraphs and underline the different verb forms. The first one has been done as an example.

13-year old's plans to stand on the top of the world!

Jordan Romero, a 13 year-old American, <u>has</u> his sights on one of the Wonders of the World, not for his geography homework, but for his own very real goal – climbing it. He wants to reach the summit of Mount Everest, in an attempt to become the youngest person who has conquered the mountain.

Jordan, along with his parents, will attempt the climb. Mt Everest is part of Jordan's ambition to bag the tallest peaks on each of the seven continents. He told his dad about what he would like to do. His dad didn't try to talk him out of it. He just explained the difficulties and what he would have to do and they started training right away.

2 Now complete the second paragraph with an appropriate form of the verbs in brackets.

His parents are no ordinary parents; they (0) ...*are*..... pro-adventure racers; that's an endurance sport that (1) .... (combine) paddling, climbing, and biking races in wilderness areas across the globe. So you see, the whole family has the bug; they see this natural wonder and want to conquer it!

Jordan (2) .... (inspire) by a school mural which depicted the seven highest summits in the world. He distinctly remembers (3) .... (see) it at the age of nine, and this is what got him (4) .... (start) on his mountaineering quest. He was the youngest American, aged 10, (5) .... (climb) the highest summit, the 19,340-foot Mount Kilimanjaro, in Africa. When he was 11 he (6) .... (add) 7,310-foot Mount Kosciusko in Australia and Europe's 18,510-foot Mount Elbrus to his accomplishments. And next on his list is Mount Everest.

However, there are those within the mountaineering community (7) .... (express) concerns about the short-term and long-term effects of high altitude on a still-developing young body.

Extreme conditions such as cold, avalanches and falls have (8) .... (face) on Everest. Temperatures near the summit (9) .... (know) to plummet 100 degrees below zero and gale-force winds blow throughout the year. There is no room for error. Mistakes often (10) .... (result) from exhaustion and even the most experienced climbers can make them.

3 Complete the gaps in the final paragraph with one word only.

Jessica Milton, a climbing historian, (1) .... not favour age limits on climbs, (2) .... she sees the trend of younger and younger climbers attempting the big mountains (3) .... a growing concern. She explains that teenage physiques are still developing, and equally (4) .... not more importantly, their reflexes based on experience have not (5) .... time to be well developed. She believes that (6) .... are good reasons (7) .... many countries have age limits for people wanting to tackle these highest summits. She gives the example of (8) .... 14-year-old who had to get a court order in Argentina (9) .... he could climb their highest peak, Aconcagua.

Adding to the challenge is the fact that Jordan's team (10) .... be attempting the summit (11) .... the help of a professional guide service, (12) .... would double expedition costs. They plan to take three sherpas for the summit attempt, as well as food and oxygen.

The team is aware of the controversy this decision (13) .... created within the climbing community. Nevertheless, they defend (14) ...., saying that what Jordan and the whole team learn and gain (15) .... the experience outweighs that.

G → Student's Book page 174

Vocabulary

1 Read this holiday advert. Underline any adjectives or phrases that have a positive connotation.

Spend a fortnight cruising down this famous and spectacular river on a luxury ship, eating delicious and varied meals in our two first-class restaurants.

Sleep in spacious and well-designed cabins, each with its own large porthole so that you can enjoy the amazing views of the river bank from the comfort of your own space. We will have frequent stops so that you can explore the many fascinating towns along the river. Whenever we stop you will be able to go on an excursion. Most of these involve no additional costs but, where there is an extra cost, rest assured that it will be extremely cheap. We guarantee that your river cruise with us will be the holiday of a lifetime that you have always dreamed of!

2 Match words from the article (1–8) with their opposites (a–h).

1	luxury	a	bland
2	delicious	b	cramped
3	varied	c	unaffordable
4	spacious	d	dull
5	large	e	tiny
6	frequent	f	budget
7	fascinating	g	monotonous
8	cheap	h	irregular

3 Read this email to a friend, describing how the holiday really was. Rewrite the <u>underlined</u> parts so they are correct or more appropriate for an informal letter.

Hi Tanya,

I've just got back from my so-called luxury cruise. OK, the river was really gorgeous with beautiful forests and castles on its banks, but as for the rest of the trip … well! In two weeks I've lost about 5 kilos **(1)** <u>due to</u> the food was far from being 'delicious'. It wasn't served in 'first-class' restaurants – more like budget class. The brochure also said that the food would be varied, but we basically had salad and pasta every day! It was so bland and monotonous.

The **(2)** <u>accomodation</u> was no better. Before we went we'd been told that the rooms were 'spacious' with a large porthole. Well, **(3)** <u>if you would have seen mine</u>, you'd realise that 'cramped' might have been a better description. **(4)** <u>With regards to</u> the porthole, it was tiny. I'd been **(5)** <u>looking forward to get off</u> the ship but there weren't as many stops as I'd been **(6)** <u>led</u> believe and the places where we did stop were some of the less interesting places. It was a bit dull, to be honest. Again, **(7)** <u>we had been promised visiting</u> many fascinating towns. And what's even worse, the brochure said that most of the excursions would be 'extremely cheap', but it **(8)** <u>turned into</u> that we **(9)** <u>must</u> pay for most of them and they were completely unaffordable.

The brochure said it would be a holiday of a lifetime – well, at least that's true in the sense it was the worse holiday I've even been on! **(10)** <u>I wish</u> that I never have another holiday like this one!

Anyway, hope things have been better for you!

Katy

1 ....
2 ....
3 ....
4 ....
5 ....
6 ....
7 ....
8 ....
9 ....
10 ....

Writing

1 Do the writing task below. Write your answer in 220–260 words in an appropriate style.

You have just returned from a holiday that failed to live up to its description in the travel company's brochure. You have decided to write a letter of complaint to the travel company. Your letter should explain why you were attracted to the holiday when you read the brochure. You should also describe how the holiday failed to meet your expectations and what you would like the company to do to compensate you.

Write your **letter**.

Under the weather

Listening

1 **1 20** Listen to five people talking about climate change. Choose the point of view which each person expresses. There are three extra opinions you do not need.

a The implications of climate change are not always what you might expect.

b Research into climate change is less conclusive than some people claim.

c Climate change may bring some advantages.

d People talk too much about climate change and neglect other environmental problems.

e International organisations are not doing enough to combat climate change.

f Each individual should do all they can to reduce their carbon footprint.

g The younger generation has a more responsible attitude to climate change than their parents.

h Claims about climate change have been exaggerated.

2 Complete the table based on words from the recording.

Noun	Verb	Adjective
	fluctuate	
cycle		
	reduce	
implication		
	minimise	
	co-operate	
	improve	
		significant
	exaggerate	
	intend	
	consider	
	inherit	

Vocabulary

1 Choose the most appropriate word in each sentence.

1 The *co-operative / cumulative* effect of decades of industrial development has resulted in global warming.

2 It's likely to flood if there is *enormous / torrential* rain.

3 According to the forecast, there will be a *heat / warm* wave next week.

4 It doesn't usually get *under / below* freezing around here.

5 If we want to combat climate change, then there has to be political *commitment / consideration*.

6 Flying less will help reduce your carbon *footprint / footstep*.

7 The ice caps are *melting / warming* at an increasing rate.

8 *Drought / Dry* is common in hot countries with no rain.

2 Complete these sentences with words from Listening exercise 2.

1 Temperatures in this country .... according to the season.

2 We are doing everything we can to .... the impact of the oil spill.

3 According to some climate change sceptics, the threat of global warming has been greatly ....

4 I'm trying to .... my carbon footprint by using the car less.

5 Whatever happens, our grandchildren will .... the world we live in.

6 There has been very little .... between the two countries to reduce carbon emissions.

7 There has been a .... increase in temperatures over the last few decades.

8 I've no .... of changing just because some people believe in climate change.

9 The whole matter needs to be given careful ....

10 Banning cars from the city centre would probably be an .... as far as air quality is concerned.

Interpreting and comparing

1 Look at this chart, which shows changes in average global temperatures over a period of about 130 years. The zero on this chart is the mean temperature from 1961–1990. Tick the connecting words in the box which could be appropriate to use when comparing things such as the temperatures in this graph.

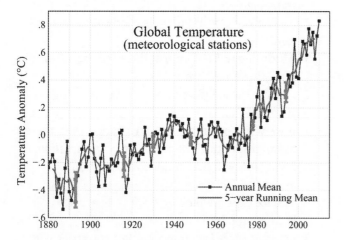

so	whereas	thereby	in addition
on the other hand		while	to sum up
in contrast	consequently		however
further	although		moreover

2 Choose the correct options.

1 A *gradual / rapid* decline is a quick change.
2 A *minimal / marked* rise is a significant change.
3 A *steep / slight* drop is a noticeable change.
4 Fluctuations are *rises / falls / falls and rises*.
5 A *steady / sudden* reduction is a gradual change.

3 Write a 220–260 word report describing the information shown in the graph. Try to use some of the words from the boxes and connecting words from exercise 1.

minimal	slight	small	gradual	steady
marked	significant	steep	sharp	rapid
sudden				

increase	rise	fluctuation	decrease	decline
fall	drop	reduce	reduction	

4 ◉ The *Cambridge English Corpus* shows that advanced learners often make mistakes with these words: *and, or, but*. Correct these sentences, written by exam candidates.

1 You will find public telephones both in the airport and in the station but also in the streets.

....

2 There was no special service or the food was not especially great.

....

3 We can stay at home without seeing anybody and speaking to a 'real' person for ages.

....

4 If someone does not feel good mentally, feels lonely, he will not work well.

....

5 I hope you will find the programme very lively sociable.

....

6 I'd like to find work in an insurance company and a bank.

....

5 Correct the wrong connecting words. Sometimes there is more than one possible answer.

1 Even he doesn't like the course, he is studying because he has to.

....

2 On the first evening, they organised a guided tour for the tourists therefore it would be a good introduction to the city for them.

....

3 However the itinerary was well planned, everything was ruined by that coach, which stopped working on Wednesday.

....

4 During travelling from the airport to the train station, I lost my baggage.

....

5 Day two was supposed to be at a typical English restaurant, while it was really at a hamburger restaurant.

....

6 You will be provided with exercise books. Although, sometimes you will need to buy extra ones.

....

G → Student's Book page 174

Reading and Use of English

1 Read the text below. Use the word given in capitals at the end of some of the lines to form a word that fits in a gap in the same line. There is an example at the beginning [0].

Climate and character

Some people believe that the climate of a country has a

(0) _significant_ impact on the character of its **SIGNIFY**

(1) .... They **INHABIT** claim, for example, that people living in extreme climates are better

equipped **(2)** .... **PSYCHOLOGY** to cope with all the

(3) .... that they **HARD** encounter in life. It is similarly claimed that people who live in lands with mild temperatures have a more

(4) .... attitude **RELAX** to life than people who come from regions that

are **(5)** .... cold. **DESPAIR**

But can climate really have an effect on someone's

(6) ....? **PERSON** Surely we should not give climate a

(7) .... role in **PROPORTION** character formation? After all, our upbringing and our genes undoubtedly have a far

more **(8)** .... role **INFLUENCE** to play.

2 Complete the second sentence so it has a similar meaning to the first, using the word given. Do not change the word given. You must use between three and six words, including the word given.

1 I think it is unlikely that there will be any improvement in the situation.
LIKELIHOOD
I think .... the situation improving

2 The committee will have to consider many factors before coming to a decision.
ACCOUNT
The committee will have to .... before coming to a decision.

3 The number of cars on the road has increased a lot in the last few decades.
SIGNIFICANT
There has been .... number of cars on the road in the last few decades.

4 According to the chart, there was a sharp rise in temperatures after 1980.
ROSE
The chart shows that .... after 1980.

5 It's not easy to significantly reduce your carbon footprint.
REDUCTION
Unfortunately, ... your carbon footprint isn't easy.

23 | I really must insist

Reading and Use of English

1 For questions 1–8, read the text below and think of the word which best fits each gap. Use only one word in each gap.

Dear Sir or Madam,

I am writing to express my deep dissatisfaction **(0)** ......*with*...... my return journey from Costa Rica on flight 4508 from San José.

As you are **(1)** .... doubt aware, there were problems with the flights on the 19th, 20th and 21st of January. I will, however, add my own comments.

(2) .... already travelled for five hours to the airport in San José, I was disappointed to find that there was a four-hour delay of my flight. However, I accepted this **(3)** .... being part of the travel experience. Your representative was supposed to give delayed passengers some vouchers for food and drink while they were waiting, **(4)** .... did not. The information regarding the flight then changed and we were told that we would **(5)** .... taking off 'in an hour or so' on a different plane. We went through to the departure lounge and continued waiting for hours, but no further information was given.

At 9 o'clock, the shops and cafeteria closed, leaving many passengers **(6)** .... any form of refreshments.

(7) .... some of these factors might have been out of your control, it was still your responsibility to make sure that passengers were kept informed, and were comfortable.

I look forward **(8)** .... your prompt reply and details of the compensation you are able to offer.

Yours faithfully,

Mrs A. Daniels

Vocabulary

1 The letter of complaint included the collocation *deep dissatisfaction*. Match each word in 1–10 with a word in a–j to make a common collocation.

1	inadequately	**a**	true
2	greatly	**b**	delayed
3	excruciatingly	**c**	inaccurate
4	promptly	**d**	informed
5	inexcusably	**e**	dull
6	awfully	**f**	investigated
7	unavoidably	**g**	inconvenienced
8	fully	**h**	sorry
9	undeniably	**i**	resolved
10	wildly	**j**	rude

2 Complete these formal phrases which can be found in letters of complaint.

1 It is with great .... that I find myself having to write to you concerning the amount of noise.
2 Would you be so .... as to send me some more information ...
3 I shall have no .... but to contact the manager.
4 I look forward to your .... reply.
5 I would very much .... it if you could check my order.
6 I would be .... if you could ...
7 I am writing in .... to your article in ...
8 If you require further information, please do not .... to contact me.
9 With reference to your letter .... 19 November, ...
10 I .... you will find my comments helpful.

Writing

1 Do the writing task below.

> You work for a travel company and received the letter on page 70 from Mrs Daniels. You have been asked to write a reply on behalf of the airline company. Your letter should acknowledge receipt of Mrs. Daniel's letter and apologise for the inconvenience she experienced. You should also explain that local conditions are often outside the control of your company and the airline and offer compensation.

Write your **letter** in 220–260 words.

Phrasal verbs (2)

1 Decide which answer (A, B or C) fits the gap in each sentence.

1 The airline won't pay any compensation, so I'm just going to have to .... experience!
   A put it down to
   B put down it to
   C put down to
2 We couldn't get our deposit back from the tour operator, so we will unfortunately have to .... £400.
   A write it off
   B write off it
   C write off
3 Don't .... writing your letter of complaint. The longer you leave it, the less likely it is that you will send it.
   A put it off
   B put on
   C put off
4 It was like talking to a brick wall. I just couldn't .... the hotel manager that we simply wouldn't accept a room in a state like that.
   A get across
   B get across it
   C get across to
5 I wonder how he's .... his new job.
   A getting on
   B getting on with
   C getting with

6 The fire .... in the basement, so everyone was able to evacuate the building safely.
   A broke itself out
   B broke it out
   C broke out

7 It looks like our holiday plans will .... if Andrea can't get time off work.
   A fall through
   B fall them through
   C fall through them

8 Crises seem to .... either the best or the worst in people.
   A bring off
   B bring out
   C bring in

9 I couldn't believe it when the manager of the hotel .... with a big bouquet of flowers and said how sorry he was that we had had so much trouble.
   A turned himself up
   B turned up
   C turned them up

10 It was awful at customs. I felt like a criminal being .... like that from the whole group and asked to empty out all my bags and pockets too!
   A singled off
   B singled away
   C singled out

2 Match the definitions below to the phrasal verbs in exercise 1.
   a make someone understand ....
   b fail to happen ....
   c arrive ....
   d think that a problem is caused by a particular thing ....
   e choose one thing for special attention ....
   f postpone ....
   g accept that money has been lost ....
   h make progress ....
   i something dangerous starts suddenly ....
   j emphasise a feature ....

3 ⊙ The *Cambridge English Corpus* shows that advanced learners often make mistakes with phrasal verbs. Replace the verbs in bold with a correct phrasal verb.
   1 I phoned a taxi company to **know** the average rate from the airport to the station. ....
   2 The problems started from the same moment I **went into** the coach. ....
   3 You take the number one bus and you **go down at** the 11th stop. ....
   4 You might be able to **take part at** our next event next July. ....
   5 The construction of the new blocks of flats could be **paid** by the grant the city has got. ....
   6 You should organise parties for everyone to **know** his or her colleagues. ....
   7 A new, good bus is indispensable if we **go to** a day-trip to Stratford-upon-Avon. ....

4 ⊙ The *Cambridge English Corpus* shows that advanced learners often make mistakes with phrasal verbs such as *get on, get off* and *find out*. Choose the correct options.
   1 You must go to the information desk to *find out / know* where to pick up your luggage.
   2 You can buy tickets as soon as you *get in / get on* the bus.
   3 Take this bus and only *get off / go down* when it arrives at its final stop.
   4 When you *go out of / get off* the bus, you will be on the left.
   5 Young people come from different countries and try to *get to know / find out* each other.
   6 On this course, you can *find out / learn* colloquial expressions and informal language.

G → Student's Book page 175

News and views

Reading and Use of English

1 For questions 1–8, complete the article by writing the missing words in the gaps. Use only one word for each gap.

Twitter is first with the news

When a plane made an emergency landing in New York's Hudson River, the news came (0) ....*not*........ from a reporter on a TV bulletin, but from Twitter.

A passenger on a ferry (1) .... the time, using his mobile phone, took a photo and uploaded it to the internet. Accompanying it was the simple message: 'There's a plane in the Hudson. I'm on the ferry going to pick (2) .... the people. Crazy.'

The US Airways plane found (3) .... in trouble less than a minute after taking off at 3.26 p.m. The photo appeared on the internet a mere 10 minutes (4) ...., at 3.36 p.m. The professional news outlets were slower. The New York Times managed to get the story onto (5) .... website by 3.48 p.m.

Social media – created by ordinary people, not by professional journalists – are now extremely important as an instant way of providing people (6) .... news stories such as the Hudson plane crash.

However, (7) .... is an issue with social-networking sites when it comes to non-biased and impartial reporting. Whereas most professional news sources aim to provide carefully checked and balanced coverage of events, social-networking sites have (8) ...., such concerns.

Listening

1 **1.21** Listen to a talk about citizen journalists. Complete the notes with one or two words in each gap.

Citizen journalists = ordinary people involved in collecting, (1) .... reporting and disseminating news and information.

They make use of (2) .... to help them create news items e.g. about a meeting of their local (3) .... This does not mean that (4) .... professional journalism is being rejected.

The public still want to feel confident that their news comes from trusted (5) ....

Professional news (6) .... are increasingly interested in public contributions.

Contributions from the public are said to complement standard coverage in a valuable and (7) ....way.

Most examples of citizen journalism are actually read on a professional news website, where they have already been checked and (8) .... by professional journalists.

Vocabulary

1 Match these words from the article and the recording to their definitions.

non-biased   coverage   insightful   complement
reporter   journalist   bulletin   feature

1 a short news programme on TV or radio
....

2 not showing any like or dislike based on personal opinions ....

3 an article in a newspaper or magazine, based on a particular subject ....

4 the reporting of an important event
....

5 having a clear understanding of a complicated problem or situation ....

6 a person whose job it is to discover information about news events and describe them for a newspaper, etc. ....

7 a person who writes news stories or articles
....

8 a thing which enhances or adds to something else ....

2 Match the verbs in the box with phrases 1–7 to make collocations from the recording. Sometimes there may be more than one possible answer.

lose   give   put   play   take   collect   find out

1 .... an overview
2 .... information
3 .... a video
4 .... something online
5 .... a job
6 .... what's happening
7 .... an active role

3 ⊙ The *Cambridge English Corpus* shows that advanced learners often make mistakes with collocations. Choose the correct options.

1 I had to *join / attend* several meetings today.
2 I am very glad that we could *achieve / reach* our aims.
3 I have recently *made / conducted* a survey about the services you offer.
4 The course *suits / meets* the needs of our company.
5 I would like to *draw / put* your attention to the high number of accidents recently.
6 It should not be difficult to *do / take* the first steps.

Reading and Use of English

1 Read the advert. Complete the gaps with the correct form of the words in capitals.

School of Media Studies

Are you interested in a career in (0) ......*journalism*........?   **JOURNAL**

We are offering an exciting and (1) .... new course   **INNOVATE**
for students keen to pursue a career in the news business.

This career-focused course is one of the best in the country and will
provide successful students with the (2) .... of skills   **BROAD**
that working in news demands. It is a (3) .... course   **RIGOUR**
and students have to be prepared to work extremely hard, but
those who are diligent can expect to acquire all the
(4) .... they will need to work in any aspect of the   **EXPERT**
news business.

The news business does not offer a (5) ....
career but our graduates will gain access to work that is   **STRESS**
(6) .... varied and stimulating.   **COMPARE**

For further details of the (7) .... of the course and   **CONTAIN**
for full information about entry (8) .... check out   **REQUIRE**
our website.

Connecting words

1 Choose the correct connecting words.

1 News stories are, as the term suggests, stories
what's more / as well as / and even news.

2 *Because of / Owing to / In spite of* the increase
in the number of TV stations, the number
of female newsreaders does not seem to be
increasing proportionally.

3 Intelligent *so / though / if* he is, I'm not sure
he'll make a good journalist.

4 The programme is interesting *or / wherever /
but* it seems to lack the visual quality we are
looking for.

5 Tim was a good cameraman. *Despite /
However, / Moreover*, he never made it to the
top of his profession.

6 *Whereas / As / Unless* we hadn't managed to get
to the scene in time, we missed getting the first
footage of the event.

7 *Owing to / As / Since* the fog we were unable to
film for two days.

8 She was *so / very / such* a photogenic little
girl, the programme couldn't fail to affect its
viewers' feelings.

9 It all happened *too fast to / so fast that /
as fast as* we didn't have time to get our
equipment in place.

10 *Because / Thanks to / In spite of* the
programme, the public has donated several
thousand pounds to the charity.

11 As a TV interviewer, you always need some
extra questions up your sleeve *or else / in case /
however* the interviewee dries up.

12 *No matter / However, / Although* how often
we plead with her to give us an interview, she
always declines.

13 He resigned from the station *but / although / as*
he couldn't accept their way of doing things.

14 I'm not sure I'll find the talk that interesting
but I'll come *anyway / even / still*.

15 *Whenever / Whatever / However* hard we tried,
we couldn't get the programme shown at prime
time.

G → Student's Book page 175

Reading

1 You are going to read four extracts in which psychologists discuss intelligence. For questions
1–4, choose from the psychologists A–D. The psychologists may be chosen more than once.

A Julia Hayes

It is interesting to study intelligent people, and to examine what makes
them more intelligent than their peers. One case is Cerys Parnell, who
on the surface is like most 11-year-old girls. She likes to text her friends,
learns tennis, and enjoys certain computer games. One thing which makes
Cerys stand out from the crowd, however, is that she is a certified genius.
She boasts an IQ estimated to be at a much higher level than most of the
population.

Why is this? One possible answer lies with her parentage. Her father is
a former chess champion, a highly successful lawyer, and according to one
intelligence test, ranks within the top 2% of the population. Another answer
undoubtedly lies in the way her father encourages her. He plays chess with
Cerys regularly, and both father and daughter appreciate this quality time
spent together. It seems that the more Cerys plays, the more she improves.
It would seem, also, that playing chess helps develop the brain and that
intelligent people also have the advantage of being more self-assured.

B Henrik Dimech

People have changed the way they think and share knowledge. Only a few centuries
ago, only the privileged had easy access to written information. Now, when one person
thinks something is interesting, or comes up with something new, he or she can share it
immediately, and can learn from it. One person's thoughts can offer changes for all of us.

We can look at the way popular culture has changed as people have got better at using
their brains. Computer games reward players who can think quickly and logically. Social-
networking sites allow people to instantly share ideas and interests and learn what other
people are doing and thinking. And as people enjoy these pursuits, their confidence
builds and whole societies can improve their cognitive abilities. It's for this reason that
our intellectual environment is changing – that we are becoming more intelligent than
our parents.

C Stephanie Alexander

There is research that indicates that intelligence is inherent: that the environment
is less of a factor on developing intelligence than we may have thought. For example,
two identical twins who were separated at birth were studied. They were born in
the same town, were adopted by completely different families, and they never met.
Being twins, they shared the same genes, and they both grew up to be fit, strong
teenagers. They both spent their free time playing football. Being fit and strong, they
were rather good at this sport. This made it even more enjoyable, so they played more
and got better still. Both went on to play for their school teams, trained regularly,
received coaching, and went on to play for the college team too. They gained 'physical
intelligence' and their success in competitions made them even surer of themselves.

Both of these boys started with the same genes. But simply being fit and strong
doesn't turn someone into a great football player. You won't be much good unless
you make the right choices, practise hard, and seek out good training. In the case
of the twins, they made the most of their environment and that explains how they
eventually became so successful.

D **Adam Glover**

The cognitive effects of playing video games have been described as 'impressive' in some recent scientific publications. It has been reported that gaming activities make the brain work better, and that they increase short-term memory and concentration. However, I would like to point out that these benefits are short lived and that over a person's lifetime may have no real significant positive impact. Another myth surrounding intelligence is that intelligent people are more self-assured and out-going but this is seldom the case. When a person is told they have above average intelligence they may feel that they have to prove this constantly at college, in their job, indeed in every aspect of their lives. This can result in feelings of pressure and insecurity. Family members should be aware of this possible outcome of revealing intelligence test scores especially to children who may not have the maturity to deal with this knowledge.

Which psychologist has a

1 different opinion from Hayes regarding the main reason affecting intelligence? ....

2 different view from Dimech on the role technology plays in developing intelligence? ....

3 similar view to Alexander on the importance of practice in reaching high standards? ....

4 different view to the others on the psychological benefits of being intelligent? ....

Vocabulary

1 ⊙ The *Cambridge English Corpus* shows that advanced learners often make spelling mistakes with words like *environment*, *intellectual* and *available*. Tick the correct words below and rewrite the mistakes.

1 appropiate ....
2 definately ....
3 begining ....
4 convenient ....
5 business ....
6 accomodation ....
7 negotiate ....
8 succesful ....
9 carreer ....
10 always ....
11 forward ....
12 healty ....
13 dissapointed ....
14 committee ....

Complex sentences and adverbial clauses

1 **Correct these sentences if necessary.**

1 He'll show the new office junior how to do.
2 What he told you was in strict confidence.
3 Is that the man you investigated?
4 This is the marketing manager, who's office is just down the corridor.
5 Who I can't stand are people which complain about everything.
6 I think I've found a time where we can both meet.
7 They'll deliver it anywhere you want.
8 That's the page whose content we'll have to change.
9 Have you interviewed the woman who's published a book about the prince?
10 That's the man who he will appear in court tomorrow.

2 **Match the beginnings of these sentences, 1–6, with the endings, a–f.**

1 I had been on holiday to the village
2 They became good friends
3 We couldn't go out at night
4 Although my sister lives in the US,
5 I always have the duck
6 Chris managed to open my car door

a unless my brother came with us.
b by forcing the window down and then reaching the latch from the inside.
c I phone her at least once a week.
d where my husband was born.
e whenever I go to that restaurant.
f because they shared many interests.

3 Combine the sentences to make one new sentence, including a relative clause.

1 Advertising is an industry. It wields considerable power within Western societies.

....

....

2 This article is by Kathy Myers. She is the editor of one of the top women's magazines.

....

....

3 The final chapter of the book will be expanded. It deals with the change in attitudes to opera.

....

....

....

4 That's Mr Williams. I was talking to him just yesterday.

....

....

....

5 Some people still speak the local dialect. A few of them live in the villages in the foothills.

....

....

6 Our research into language has produced some interesting results. The most interesting ones show that as many new words are coming into the language as old ones that are dying out.

....

....

7 We listened to recordings of several dialects. I'd never heard many of them before.

....

....

8 There were two fantastic photos for the book. One was chosen as the front cover.

....

....

4 ⊙ The *Cambridge English Corpus* shows that advanced learners often make mistakes with sentences using words like *who*, *what* and *which*. Correct these sentences written by exam candidates.

1 One member has also complained about your booking system, that should be improved urgently.

....

2 The aim of this report is to suggest a magazine for students who they would like to study Greek.

....

3 I want to give you information about my neighbour which I have known for a long time.

....

4 The opening hours are from eight o'clock, what are perfect.

....

5 The exchange students, that will be visiting you from July, do not require special food.

....

Ⓖ→ Student's Book page 176

Use of English

1 Complete the second sentence so it has a similar meaning to the first sentence. Do not change the word given. You must use between three and six words, including the word given.

1 The girl said she regretted paying so little attention in class.
WISHED
The girl said she .... attention in class.

2 The teacher said that no one could justify behaving so badly.
NO
The teacher said there .... for such bad behaviour.

3 Every time I take an IQ test, I panic and can't think.
WHENEVER
I panic and become unable .... an IQ test.

4 Just because he's intelligent, it doesn't mean he never does anything stupid.
EVEN
Unfortunately, ... intelligent, it doesn't mean he never does anything stupid.

5 There was little sign of improvement in Linda's piano playing even though she practised every day.
DESPITE
There was little sign of improvement in Linda's piano playing .... every day.

Recording scripts

Unit 2

1 01

M: What are you doing?

F: Look at this. My grandad just joined Facebook.

M: Your grandad?

F: Yeah. He sent me a message. Look.

M: Hey Maria. What's up? I'm on Facebook now. LOL! That's your grandad? How old is he?

F: It's just wrong! My grandad shouldn't write 'What's up'! He definitely shouldn't write 'LOL!'

M: Why not! He just wants to get his message across. It's only chat. That's what people do, isn't it? It would be more weird if he wrote 'Dear Maria, I hope this email finds you well ...'

F: I guess so. That's the point, it's an alternative to talking face-to-face. So it doesn't have to be so formal.

M: Yeah – it's the style. I mean in work, if I have to write something formally or just write properly, I will.

F: Yeah, I guess people have got into the habit of just typing like they're speaking.

M: Nothing wrong with that. Trouble is, some people might look down on you and think your English isn't good if you always write like that.

F: Yeah – you've got to adapt your style to the situation, depending on what you're doing.

M: Well, if your grandad can do it send him a reply. Teach him some more phrases!

1 02

M: Have you seen that survey? The one about living life to the full?

F: Yes. I found the introduction especially useful. It was really well written and it clearly outlined the methodology used for the survey and what it covers. I ended up spending the whole weekend going through it and making notes.

M: Really? I was thinking I might use it in some of my lectures.

F: That's a good idea. I'm sure your students will get a lot out of it.

M: Hopefully. I'm doing something next week on how people make use of their free time and what influences their decisions about how to spend it.

F: Well, this survey should be pretty useful, then. If I were you, I'd mention how it classified people as risk-takers and so on, and then examined their lifestyles. How it confirmed that people who think positively are very balanced – their days are a good balance of work and home life.

M: Good idea.

F: One thing which struck me, in the survey, was that people who plan ahead carefully, you know, people who make schedules, and organise their time, they can actually achieve a lot more than they thought possible. I'd imagine that most people assume risk takers live life more to the full. But actually, it seems that the reverse is true.

1 03

F: Peter, do you know what you're going to do after your degree? Are you thinking of doing a postgrad course? Or it'd be nice to go travelling for a few months, wouldn't it?

M: Well yes, but I did that before coming to uni. And you did, too, didn't you?

F: Yes, I was in Asia for a couple of months. Actually, what I'm hoping to do is get on a management course. I've got a job interview next week, for a bank. I think I ought to be getting on with real life. I'm ready for that now.

M: Yeah and you'd probably get promoted pretty quickly, even without a postgrad degree.

F: Yeah, and going straight on to do another course doesn't seem like the right thing to do at the moment.

M: Yeah.

F: And you know, it's good to get out of studying and do something different. I think I could learn a lot of new things at work. I always want to make sure I have an inquisitive attitude, keep up my thirst for knowledge. But I can do that in the workplace – I don't need to spend all my life in a university.

M: Sure. You know, I always look up to people who never stop learning. The only thing I'm afraid of is I think I might turn out to be a workaholic, so I need to make sure I schedule in free time too so that there's a balance.

F: Yes, sure. Work shouldn't end up taking over your whole life. I can still go travelling in my holidays!

Unit 3

1 04

My name is Dr Ron Adams, and today I'll be talking about how people react to finding themselves suddenly in the public eye.

There have been several cases recently where a young person has gained overnight fame. Without warning, people begin recognising them in the street. There's a tricky balancing act between seeking publicity and a desire to maintain a sense of privacy. Interestingly, famous people initially experience a sense of isolation, as they find it difficult to keep in touch with their old friends. Any feeling of freedom, which their fame and fortune can undoubtedly buy, only comes with time.

If a well-known person finds it difficult to be in the public eye, there is a temptation to leave the urban community they live and work in, and opt for life in a rural community. However, I'd warn against this because, in fact, it's easier to pass unnoticed in a busy city street.

It is a great pity that many famous people become unhappy when they attain a celebrity status. In my opinion, it's photographers who are mainly responsible for this rather than journalists. If a journalist pushes a microphone in front of an actor and asks a question, the actor's aware of what's going on. However, it's not the same with a telephoto lens. The resulting shots, which can often be very embarrassing, can even lead to a fear of going out in public. Some famous people employ bodyguards to protect them, although this is more common among some female stars, and it certainly isn't the norm. What we are seeing more of though, are personal assistants, who take over most of the day-to-day running of a celebrity's life. While this is a very practical solution to many of the problems the rich and famous face, it can have some unexpected outcomes. I don't mean that the celebrity loses his or her independence or even self-confidence – no – what happens is that they actually have less creativity than they had before.

Of course, there are many different types of famous people, there are actors, singers, musicians and so on, and then there are politicians, even news broadcasters, and they do seem to react differently to being famous. News readers often don't cope well with being interviewed by the press about non-news issues; they don't believe they have any claim to fame. Sports people, on the other hand, seem to enjoy their sporting successes being made public. Because of their training, they know how to keep focused and rarely answer interviewers' questions if they don't want to. They know it's not in the public interest, or indeed in their interest, to talk about their private lives.

It's also worth pointing out that how famous people are portrayed is often down to them. I wish they'd think more carefully about their behaviour when they're out in public. They shouldn't do anything which will give the press something they can build up to portray a certain image of that person. Once someone has, for example, a reputation for being rude, it's very hard to get rid of it. As ordinary members of the public, we'll never realise the amount of mental, as opposed to physical, stress that celebrities are under as a result of this constant exposure. And we should think twice before wishing we were famous.

Unit 4

1 05

Hi, in my talk this morning I'm going to give you an overview about choosing a university or college and I'm basing the information on my own experience. I'll go through what I think are the most important criteria, and we'll have time at the end for questions.

When I first started looking seriously at going to university in the UK, I drew up a list of about six places that interested me. I knew that I wanted to study Journalism, but beyond that, I was pretty open-minded about which university I should go to. Like you, I was in my last year of high school, and I was living with my parents in the north-east of England. I showed my list of universities to my parents. It was interesting because I thought they'd focus on course fees as they would be helping me out financially if and when necessary, but it was the location of the university I'd put at the top of the list that bothered them. They pointed out that it would take about seven hours for me to get home from there. So I revised my list.

All universities hold open days for prospective students and these are really helpful. You get to meet various people, tutors and students of course, and you can ask any questions you like. Prepare questions before you go so that you don't forget anything. I found the social programme officers the most useful to talk to in terms of getting a real feel of what it would be like to be a student at the university. So once you think you know which university you'd like to go to, you must check the course. You have to make sure that the modules on offer are suitable for you – and while reading the module overview is one thing, you have to study the unit guide to get the details you need to be able to make your decision.

I eventually decided on Salford University. The Journalism course they offer is exactly what I was looking for. And another thing you should do is find out about the tutors you'll be working with. I was fascinated by a research paper one of my tutors had written, and when I was looking at different universities, I saw that some tutors had written really famous books.

So once you've found the course for you, don't forget to think carefully about money. You need to add up the course fees and the cost of course materials. Then check out the cost of living of the city where the university is. I used one of those comparison websites for that and it was really accurate and gave me a good idea of how much I'd need per month. Then you have to think about how you're going to fund your studies. You can get a student loan from a bank and most students need to supplement that with work, if they don't want to tighten their belts too much. I was really pleased that I'd checked out the employment situation around Salford. It was good and meant that during holidays I could earn some money.

I know it may seem like a trivial thing, but most students don't think about checking it out and that's the gender balance at the university. Prospective students spend hours finding out about facilities but don't think so much about who they'll actually be studying with – and of course partying with. I've really enjoyed working with the girls on some of my projects; they've brought a different perspective to them.

And on a slightly related subject, it's really important to know the kind of accommodation that the uni can offer you. That can make a huge difference in your first year especially. If you can live on campus, you'll make friends quickly and soon feel at home if you've moved to a new city.

Unit 5

1 06

Speaker 1: I've been living and working here for about three years now and love it. I think it's a real privilege to be working as a tour guide – you get to meet a lot of new people all the time of course, but what I love is the fact that we have to explore the region, you know get right off the beaten track and look for new experiences for the tourists. I can't believe, looking back on it now, that I complained about trivial things when I came out here, and was worried about lots of things. Although cooked breakfasts did take some getting used to, it all seems perfectly natural now!

Speaker 2: I work with people who book package tours, and they really make me work for my money! You can't believe the things they ask me! They think I'm a walking encyclopedia! Actually, it's the best part of the job though, finding out new facts. I take them round all the main attractions, meet up with them back at the hotel. I never get a minute to myself and that was really hard for the first couple of months. For tomorrow, I've organised a trip where we have to take a bus and then a boat, then horses until we get to the picnic spot in the forest.

Speaker 3: There's never a dull moment. Some people think you're only busy in the summer, that that's the peak season, but in fact, most tourist destinations are busy all year round now. Now that I can speak Portuguese almost fluently, things are great. It was a nightmare, when I first came here – it was hard to make myself understood. But now I spend all my free time with the people who live in the town, and that's what makes it for me. I feel part of this community.

Speaker 4: When I found out that I was being posted here, I wasn't exactly over the moon. It's got a reputation as a tourist trap and because of that, people said there was a lot of pick-pocketing and things. So I was really scared at first. But I soon discovered it wasn't even true. I've been here for a year now and I've learnt the language and I've learnt to drive. If you can't do that, it's hard to get around. I love meeting these challenges. Next I'm going to try to persuade a local restaurant to give us special rates!

Speaker 5: Well I certainly didn't expect to be living on this island for two years, but it's so wonderful, I extended my contract. Hoards of tourists flock here every summer in search of sun, sand and fun. And I'm not surprised – it's amazing. There are the usual attractions, plus a lot more if you go into the hills. Partly because the island's volcanic, the hills and beaches have a special quality which you can't find elsewhere. It does get really hot in summer and that seemed unbearable at first but I've acclimatised and make sure I don't do anything too energetic around midday.

Unit 6

1 `07`

In today's edition of *Language Today*, we look at how text messaging has created a new language, bypassing conventional spelling and grammar rules to the despair of some traditionalists. Text-messaging is amazingly convenient. Imagine this: you're sitting on a bus rushing to meet a friend. You're late. So you get out your phone and, to avoid having an argument, or an irritating *I'M ON THE BUS* conversation, you tap in the letters I-L space B space L followed by the number 8. Then press send. Why don't we make the effort to spell out the words in full? Well, text messages, also known as SMS (short message service), were originally restricted to 160 characters.

The rather tedious method of typing in letters using the phone keypad also means the shorter the words, the less frustrating they are to type. There's also the not insignificant point, of course, that making contact via a text message is a lot cheaper than making a voice call.

Text messaging is not a minority activity – it's estimated that by 2008 over 4.1 trillion SMS were sent. Mobile phone companies seemed to have been caught completely off guard. So if anybody tells you that they predicted the success of text messaging, don't believe them. The first text message was sent in 1992, and the service became commercially available in 1993. It was initially slow to catch on. Today, religious leaders are texting to call their congregations to prayer; doctors text advice to their parents; and shops text special offers on cut-price jeans.

The trend has also helped thousands of relationships in their early stages, as text messaging is so much less embarrassing than an awkward telephone call.

There are no rules to text messaging. It is a vital, evolving language full of phonetic abbreviations. The short, informal style of an email is cut down even further by the mini-missives in a text message. We are opening up a new channel of playful, frank, 24-hour communication and this is having a huge impact on our language. Behind this electronic shorthand, a cultural revolution is brewing. In this language soup, what is happening to good old-fashioned English?

One linguistics expert has commented that text messaging is fun but there seem to be worries about the effects it might be having on children's literacy. He has noticed a sharp decline in the writing that his university students produce.

If future generations prefer to text message rather than learn to read and write, things won't improve. In the future, it might be that writing changes into something completely different, just as it has done over the past 50 years with the growth of telephones and the internet.

However, not everyone shares this nervousness about text messaging and its detrimental influence on children.

One professor of language and communication has made the point that playing with language is entirely natural. She says that every time a new medium comes along, it has an effect on language. Over the past few decades, language has changed quickly because of the way people use new technologies. She believes this doesn't destroy the existing language. On the contrary, it helps language evolve. In text messages, many words come from shorthand created in email, such as FYI (for your information) and IMO (in my opinion). Most of these are original, although there is sometimes an initial clash of meanings. For example, 'LOL' can mean both 'Laughing Out Loud' and 'Lots Of Love'. Who knows what embarrassing misunderstandings this might have created.

One of the most ubiquitous uses of text messages is to assist in the process of new relationships. When falling in love, the mobile phone becomes a valuable friend. Unlike Shakespeare, who crafted poetry using a quill and paper, today's lovers are more likely to send a text.

So what do you think? Text us your ideas on …

Unit 8

1.08

Although online courses aren't the perfect learning situation for everyone, the number of such classes seems to be increasing every year. Unfortunately, this is not always because of positive reasons. Many institutions of higher learning see distance courses as money-saving and many students often think distance learning will be easier. But colleges and students are mistaken if they think these ideas are true. Online courses don't require actual classrooms, but they do need extensive software and training systems. As someone with many years of experience as an online course developer, I can state with absolute certainty that distance education is at least as hard work as face-to-face learning. So what should you do if you're preparing to do an online course and want to make the most of it? Well, the first thing is that there is always a tutorial on the software used by the institution. Students need to take advantage of this and familiarise themselves with the software they're going to be using. If a book about studying online is recommended, make sure you get a copy. What you learn will save you time in the long run. Speaking of time, managing it is the number one issue that online students must tackle. If a student's the type who waits until the last minute to prepare assignments or read textbooks for class, he or she may very likely be in trouble in an online environment.

The best action to take if you are enrolled in an online class is to create a timetable for yourself and put it somewhere you will see it (like your bedroom door, if necessary). Check the online class webpage every day, if possible, to keep up with discussions and any other messages. Just because you're taking a class online doesn't mean it's only 'you and your computer'. There are other students in a class and you will probably be frustrated if you don't have any contact with them. Research has been conducted indicating that social interaction is very important to online students. Therefore, if the instructor doesn't suggest that you introduce yourself at the beginning of the class (he or she should), do so anyway by sharing a few personal details about yourself, including why you're taking the class and what you hope to get out of it. Other students will likely respond to you and you may have some 'study friends' for the future, even if communication is through email. It's also a good idea to introduce yourself to the instructor. This can just be a succinct email message. A considerate note such as this can make you stand out and impress him or her with your social skills. Most students say little or nothing to a teacher until it's the end of a course and they're in trouble. At the beginning of this talk, I mentioned students who forget to come to class when they take a distance course. There are some students who do the opposite, suffering from 'over-attending'. Enthusiastic about making contributions and keen to receive responses to their comments, these students can't stay away from an online discussion board. An example was an eager student from one of my graduate classes – I'll call him John – who found himself checking the course area about six times a day. John also got involved in lengthy email exchanges with several of his classmates. That was fine except that John nearly forgot about the rest of his life (yes, this actually happened!) and started suffering headaches from staring at a computer screen for hours and hours. John's boss was not pleased when she found him working on responses for the class discussion board when he was at work, and John's wife was furious that he got so consumed by his computer course that he stayed up half the night.

Online learning is still relatively new to the scene of higher education and is still being developed. If you find that you are going to be a virtual student (or are helping a virtual student), try to learn as much as you realistically can about the online environment and take precautions, especially figuring out how to manage your time.

Unit 9

1.09

Dan: Have you ever lived in a megacity?

Maria: I'm not sure really? Does London count as a megacity?

Dan: It certainly does. So you've lived there, then?

Maria: Yes, for about three years when my parents were working there. What about you?

Dan: Oh, I'm a country boy. This is the largest place I've ever lived in and it's a town, not even a city, let alone a megacity. But I visited Shanghai on my gap year. That was amazing.

Maria: Oh, I'd love to go there. I read a novel set there once which had a huge impact on me.

Dan: It's certainly a very impressive place.

Maria: My brother's just got a new job in a megacity – New York. That sounds a very exciting place – people seem to live at a much faster pace there.

Dan: I'm not sure I could cope with that. Or having to spend at least an hour every day commuting to work on a crowded subway. And I think the noise would get me down too.

Maria: I think I could get used to all of that. It'd be the fact that you'd be very unlikely to know your neighbours that I'd find hardest to live with. I don't think you'd have the same feeling of belonging in a place that you do when you live somewhere smaller and can't go out without bumping into someone you know and stopping to pass the time of day with them.

Dan: Yes, I agree. That's what would really stop me from moving somewhere like New York, unless I absolutely had to.

1.10

F: Is it true you're considering moving to the country, John?

M: Sure. I've been thinking about it for a while. The wife and kids have taken a bit of persuading, but they've come round to the idea now.

F: I guess it means you can afford a bigger house?

M: Absolutely. And I've got really keen on growing my own fruit and veg. That's my main motivation for leaving the city. I've only got a window box here.

F: But won't you miss the city? You've lived here all your life, haven't you?

M: Yes, but it's not like I go to the theatre or cinema much these days. I'd have missed those much more if I'd left in my 20s. I know I've been spoilt by living on a 24-hour bus route and not having that will take a bit of getting used to. My wife says she'll miss the shops but that won't be a problem for me, I don't think.

F: Well, you can order most things you want online.

1 11

M: Stowton has changed so much over the last ten years, hasn't it!

F: I guess so. It hasn't grown quite as much as other towns round here, though, has it?

M: I'm not sure about that. There's that huge development to the north of the river, don't forget.

F: Oh, yes, of course. I'm amazed the city planners gave permission to build there. There used to be such a beautiful park.

M: Well, I'm sure they must have been torn over what to do. More housing was needed somewhere and someone or other would have raised objections, wherever they allowed it to be built.

F: Yes, I wouldn't have wanted to be in their shoes.

M: So would you say most of the changes are for the better?

F: I'm not sure. It's certainly a much livelier place to live now.

M: Yes, but the traffic congestion is horrific.

F: Well, there are certainly some negatives, but on reflection I guess I'd come down on the positive side.

M: I'm not sure I'd agree with you there.

Unit 10

1 12

It goes without saying that Charlie and I love each other and want to grow old together. Our commitment is already made. In a sense, there is no reason to get married at all. Which meant that I was taken aback when he first suggested it to me. In fact, I rejected the idea. But then I began to think about it and to take on board his arguments. I re-examined my objections. I began to suspect that by getting married, I wouldn't actually, really, be supporting (still less exposing myself to) female servitude.

Once I began to think of marriage as a possible choice out of many possible choices, and not something imposed on me, it didn't seem quite so awful after all. Plus, even if cold-light-of-day statistics said that we had as much chance of failing as making it work till death us do part, so what? Why bother at all, if you refuse to try things you might fail at? Once I had got rid of the objections, I started to be able to see certain advantages. That a wedding really could be a celebration of partnership, friendship and family ties. (Admittedly putting two sets of families and a bunch of our friends in the same room could be a huge disaster.) That we

actually do, really do, have a strange urge to tell everybody that we love each other and it might be nice to give our family and friends a good party while we're at it.

It surprises me to say this, but we actually do want to do the ritual thing. We want to do as our forefathers did before us, in a place hallowed by time. As you will by now be grasping, I also started to think how immensely romantic it would be to get married. And I know that romance is a literary invention, but well, I really don't mind any more. So we're getting married in a church near my parents' home and doing everything 'properly'. Well, mostly everything. I'm not going for white, but a simple green. I have not darkened the door of a single store's bridal department (in fact the word 'bridal' still makes me shudder). I'm not wearing a veil or having bridesmaids, but I shall be making a speech. There won't be any wedding cake, or morning suits, or formal photographs, or a Rolls-Royce (my eldest brother is polishing up his 50s Citroën DX). I shan't be going up the aisle to the traditional music, but to something postmodern by my oldest friend, a composer. I certainly hope there won't be any pomposity or smugness. It's not exactly revolutionary, but it's a way of making it ours. Which is kind of what we're hoping for in our marriage, too.

Unit 12

1 13

Speaker 1: I've just come back from travelling, and I'm going to start university soon. I had to decide whether or not to go travelling alone or find other people to go with. The trouble with that was I could see the advantages as well as the drawbacks of both. In the end, I went on my own rather than with a group, and in retrospect it was the right thing to do. I found out how to get by without anyone else giving me advice. My mum was really worried when I told her I was going for a month alone. But I think now she's proud of what I've done.

Speaker 2: It took ages for me to make up my mind mainly because I realised what an important decision it was. I'd studied engineering for two years but found it too demanding. The lab work took up about six to eight hours a week. Eventually, after a long chat with various friends, I swapped to business. I actually wish I'd done it earlier but I didn't like the idea of everyone knowing I wasn't coping very well. All my friends seemed to be getting along fine with whatever they'd decided to do so why couldn't I just get on with what I'd initially chosen? Anyway, the next big decision I'll have to make is to find a job. I hope that's easier!

Speaker 3: I feel as though I've just run a marathon and I know what that's like because I used to belong to a running group! No, it's official, as of last Monday I'm now regional sales rep; one up from sales team leader. The interview process was long. I had a panel interview, where in addition to other questions, I was asked to talk about my strengths and weaknesses, and then a week later an interview with the marketing manager. What was scary about that was at the end of it, he congratulated me and asked me to confirm that I would accept by the end of the next day. I hadn't even talked it over with my parents or anything!

Speaker 4: I'm in charge of a group of people at an insurance company but I've only recently been promoted to this supervisory position. I have to give out tasks to each team member and, because I knew that some of the team preferred dealing with property insurance, others with car insurance, etc., I'd tie myself in knots attempting to give people work they'd enjoy. But it never seemed to work out. People started complaining they had more work than others. So one day, I decided just to give out the next task to the next person who was due work, irrespective of what it was. And you know what? They haven't even noticed and all my stress has just evaporated!

Speaker 5: I inherited a house from my grandmother. It was worth quite a lot of money and I sold it because it was in a completely different part of the country. And I know this sounds odd but trying to decide what to invest the money in was a nightmare. I felt as though I didn't have all the facts and figures and was terrified of making the wrong decision. I'd promised my dad that I would discuss it with him, which I did, and then the next morning I thought OK, I'm going to set up my own company with the money. And it's doing really well so now I have the courage to take on more staff and expand the company.

Unit 14

1 14

Extract 1

M: I know some people say that language is a living thing and that it's always changing, but in at least some areas of life, I believe that standards should be maintained.

F: I know, every time I read the newspaper, or start reading an article, even ones written by so-called respected journalists, you find mistakes.

M: Exactly. They should write properly, using proper, well-formed sentences. Not to write as if they're having a friendly chat with the reader. Don't these people understand that grammar is a set of rules followed by the users of a language? And with this in mind, I've compiled a list of the most important grammar rules – proper sentences, semicolons, everything – and I plan to put it online in the hope that people will finally learn how to write properly.

F: Another thing I've noticed is the trend for using lower-case letters on signs, websites, adverts – everything!

M: I suppose they think it's fashionable and that it looks more friendly.

F: But what happened to the rules of punctuation? In my opinion, it all looks the same – childish. And for that reason, I can't see it surviving.

M: I hope not!

Extract 2

F: Hi, Mike, how are you enjoying our Russian classes?

M: Hi Jennifer. I'm getting a huge amount out of them. And of course, I'm going onto lots of websites that help with pronunciation and vocabulary.

F: Yes, I look online too. I'm looking for more work on

grammar though …that's my weakness according to our teacher.

M: Oh, don't worry, everyone finds it hard. And I think our teacher's smart. She just lets everyone listen and only join in when they feel confident enough to say something. You don't feel under pressure.

F: That way of teaching works really well for me, and all of us actually, I think.

M: Yeah. So, you're learning Russian because you love the classic Russian authors, aren't you?

F: Well, I'd love to be able to read Tolstoy in Russian – perhaps one day. But the reason I took up Russian is more practical than that. I know that Russia is a fast growing economy. And who knows, one day I might be travelling round Russian cities visiting my contacts; you know, when I'm a well-established entrepreneur!

Extract 3

M: That lecture on how the human body is well-adapted for speech was great, wasn't it?

F: Yes there were lots of things that I'd never thought about like how human teeth are different to those of other animals because they're even in size and form an unbroken barrier.

M: And the top and bottom set meet.

F: And another thing was that because human lips have well developed muscles which are intricately interlaced, we can speak! The human tongue is thick, muscular and mobile, and this means that the mouth cavity can be varied so a range of vowel sounds can be produced.

M: Some of the information was new for me … the part about the human throat being much simpler than in other primates, which means air can move freely upwards and out of the mouth.

F: But one disadvantage is that breathing while eating is out of the question.

M: True, and I already knew that our breathing is well adapted to speech because we can change its pace when we speak without noticing any discomfort.

F: That was in that article we had last term, right? I liked the part of the lecture that compared the length of childhood in humans and animals.

M: Yes, humans seem to be born very early compared to other animals. And most babies only begin to speak at around the age of about nine months.

Unit 16

1 15

We can hear, see, smell, taste and touch the world around us. These five senses often provide the alarm to signal a possible danger. If we touch something painful, see or hear something frightening, smell or taste something unpleasant, evasive action is advised!

However, most of the changes or threats around us are not so obvious. These five senses can't detect everything that happens within our bodies, or all the many important changes in the environment. For that, there are hundreds of 'hidden body senses' that can operate even when we are asleep and we aren't even aware of them. Cells can detect the temperature within and outside our bodies with reasonable accuracy – they can determine the levels of oxygen and carbon dioxide in the air, in our lungs, blood and tissues, or the acidity of our bodies, and the amount of 'fuel' in the form of food stores, available. One of the responses that we're all aware of is changes in our heart rate. The heart must pump blood around the body to deliver essential oxygen and nutrients to all the cells and tissues, and remove potentially harmful waste products. It must beat continuously. The heart can respond, within a second, to a potential danger or a need within the body. When we are about to run it starts beating faster even before we begin to use our muscles, and it can adapt to training, stress and long-term needs.

Humans and animals are like sophisticated computers. Millions of pieces of information from sensors throughout the body are relayed, processed and integrated, often within the brain. The next task is activating the appropriate responses – sometimes in less than a second. All of these complicated activities are essential to keep the internal environment of the body at the optimal level state for life. Our bodies need to maintain this constant interior in order to function and survive. How we do this is a fascinating story with many chapters.

Unit 18

1 16

Man: This is a wonderful exhibition, isn't it?
Woman: Yes, it certainly is.
Man: Do you come to this gallery often?
Woman: Well, I haven't been here for a while.
Man: I particularly like this painting, don't you? It's wonderful, the way it depicts life in London in 1910 or so ... So different from how things were in the 19th century, when rich and poor people would never come together in the way they do here.
Woman: Well, yes, but …
Man: And the artist is such a master. I find his use of blue, green and black very impressive, quite different from other artists of his period. They were much more focused on conveying light and shade effectively – a technique called *chiaro scuro*, you know. But I would hate to bore you with terminology.
Woman: Well you certainly have an original take on the painting! But I'm afraid you're not quite right in some of the details. I'm actually amazed you didn't recognise this as an *Impressionist* painting? They're generally so well-known.
Man: What do you mean exactly?
Woman: Actually, I studied art in Paris and wrote a dissertation on the artist who did this painting. His name's Renoir and he took great pleasure in the city of Paris where he lived. This picture shows the *Moulin de la Galette* which was a popular place for young working-class people to go to for a Sunday afternoon dance. You can see there the courtyard, shaded by acacia trees. The effect of the light is a typical feature used by painters in the *Impressionist* school

but Renoir seems to exploit it to particular effect, wouldn't you agree? What is particularly striking about this painting is that no one before Renoir had thought of capturing aspects of daily life on such a large canvas.
Man: Oh, I see. Yes. Well, nice to have met you.
Woman: Bye!

Unit 19

1 17

In our lecture today we're going to continue looking at the psychology of human behaviour focusing on how what we do may be influenced by the way that others flatter us. Most of us pride ourselves on being able to recognise when someone is flattering us rather than giving us their sincere opinion of our new hairstyle or the decoration of our living room. If one of my students comes up to me and says 'Professor, your course has completely transformed my understanding of psychology' I at once expect this to be followed by a desperate request for an extension of an essay deadline or something along those lines.

But does flattery perhaps have an impact on a deeper level? Might it affect people who recognize that they're being flattered as well as those naïve people who are less aware of what is going on? This was the hypothesis behind a piece of research carried out recently by one of my doctoral students from Australia. She carried out her study here in Canada, basing it on some work done a few years ago in Hong Kong. Participants in the earlier study had been asked to evaluate a new department store based on one of the store's advertisements while my student chose to make a new and rather upmarket sports centre the focus of her study. She wanted to go for a place that would be mainly used by the relatively well-off to see if they were any more or less susceptible to flattery than the public at large.

The advert for the sports centre described in glowing terms what it had to offer, but it also praised readers for their intelligent approach to fitness and the attractive physiques they had acquired as a result. While the subjects of the study almost without exception recognised the advert as flattery with the ulterior motive of selling centre membership, my doctoral student was more interested in how her subjects' attitudes would be influenced at the implicit level.

In other words, she wanted to discover firstly whether subjects would develop more positive feelings towards the sports centre even though they had rejected their ad as meaningless flattery. And if so, would this implicit reaction then be a predictor of later behaviour? In other words, her main aim was to find out whether even the people who were aware of the tricks of advertisers would actually go straight to the sports centre, credit card in hand? It turns out that implicit attitudes towards the sports centre were indeed better predictors of the likelihood of applying for sports centre membership. So it seems that while participants quickly dismissed these ads at the explicit level, the flattery was exerting an important effect at a sub-conscious level.

So why are people so susceptible to flattery? There is

evidence to show that most people have a reasonably high opinion of themselves. Ask a group of people how good they are at driving, for example, and the chances are they will all consider themselves to be above average. Of course, this is statistically impossible. So, it isn't surprising that we are particularly receptive to messages consistent with such a rosy-eyed view of who we are and what we can do. We may pretend to brush it off when someone compliments us on our new jacket, but deep down we're thinking, "You know what? I do look good".

To take her study a stage further my student did an additional experiment. She instructed one group of participants to write about a personality trait that they would like to change and the other group to write about a trait that they felt positively about. As she had expected she found that engaging in self-criticism heightened the effect of flattery on implicit attitudes while self-affirmation modified this effect. In other words, people who lack a degree of self-confidence to begin with are even more than usually vulnerable to the message behind a smooth sales pitch.

Unit 20

1 18

There are many different types of places to eat. One important question is who uses different places and how often they go. As sociologists, we are initially very interested in the social and cultural characteristics of people who behave differently. Such characteristics indicate the financial, social, practical and cultural forces systematically distributed across the population, which constrain or encourage people to engage in particular ways of eating out. We asked respondents how often they ate out under different circumstances. Excluding holidays and eating at work, on average, respondents ate a main meal out about once every three weeks; 21% ate out at least once a week, a further 44% at least monthly and only 7% claimed never to eat out. The mean frequency of eating at someone else's home was about the same, but a much larger proportion (20%) never did so. Another 20% of respondents claimed never to eat in the home of other family members, and about one third never at the home of friends. Very regular eating out with either family or friends was not very prevalent, but being a guest at a main meal in someone else's home was part of the life experience of a large majority of the population. There is a strong positive association between being a guest of friends, a guest of family and eating out in restaurants. Opportunities to eat out are cumulative, particularly eating out commercially and with friends. To be seen in the right places and in attractive company, or at least to let others know that we are familiar with the most exciting or rewarding of experiences, is part of a process of display and performance which contributes to reputation. Early sociologists examining consumption were particularly interested in the claiming and attributing of status through exhibitions of a prestigious lifestyle. They were particularly concerned with the ways in which individuals established reputations for refinement,

superiority and distinction. Consumption patterns reflected social standing, and particularly class position. Eating out is a potential means for such display through the use or avoidance of different venues.

Unit 21

1 19

Speaker 1: The 'Seven Wonders of Nature' campaign is a global search to recognise the seven most wondrous natural sites in the world through the eyes of the public.

In the first stage, the public was asked to nominate the seven natural wonders of their choice. In Australia, 13 sites were listed. Two of these sites, Uluru (also commonly known as Ayers Rock) and the Great Barrier Reef have received enough support to take them through to stage two of the campaign.

These two sites successfully fought off competition from 259 other spectacular natural icons. My vote went to Uluru in Australia's Red Centre. My reasons are simple. In a nutshell, it's vibrant in colour, rich in texture and steeped in history. Uluru is the world's largest monolith, and has rightly become an icon of Australia.

The rock is over 318 metres high, 9.4 kilometres in circumference and extends six kilometres below the ground's surface. Designated a UNESCO World Heritage site since 1987, Uluru is also remarkable for its religious and spiritual significance. But these are just facts; you have to go there and see it with your own eyes to even begin to understand why I think it should be included as one of the Seven Wonders of Nature.

Speaker 2: I'm nominating Canada's Bay of Fundy for one of the 'Seven Wonders of Nature'. The Bay of Fundy is a long ocean bay that stretches between the provinces of New Brunswick and Nova Scotia on the country's east coast. Here's why I think Bay of Fundy should be on the list. The Fundy region has so many geology firsts it's almost embarrassing: the world's best fossil forest; Canada's oldest dinosaurs; the world's smallest dinosaurs; evidence of the 'missing link' between the Jurassic and Triassic periods of geological history; it's the best place in the world to see rock types from three different geological time periods: igneous, sedimentary and metamorphic.

It's the best site in the world for tidal power potential. The tides here, at 15 metres, are the highest on the planet. Then, in summer, it's the habitat and feeding ground for 12 species of whales, including the endangered North Atlantic right whale. Fundy's low-tide mud flats are a critical feeding ground for 95% of the world's sandpipers on their annual migration from the Arctic to the west coast of Africa, then South America.

Last but not least, it boasts some of the best seafood in North America: lobster, salmon, mussels, sole, edible seaweed, and so much more!

Speaker 3: The place I nominate as one of the 'Seven Wonders of Nature' is somewhere I visited as a student, some years ago. I'd flown to Santiago, where I met my guide and we travelled up into the mountains. I tried to acclimatise gradually to the altitude, on the Chilean side of the Andes. Then the day came when my guide and I left town. We negotiated the steep climb to the famous Tatio geysers. Then we went through a desert of gravel and rock, the landscape changing at every bend, and the smoking volcano, Volcan Machuca, the only constant in our sights. At 4,300 metres, we reached a plateau of some 40 geysers. Boiling underground streams met the cold morning air, sending up hissing plumes of sulphurous steam.

It was amazing to be at the salt lake, Salar de Atacama, at dusk. Its surface was jagged and dusted with sand. This salt lake harbours almost half the world's lithium – used for batteries.

Another guide arrived to take me to Bolivia. "It'll be different," he claimed. And he was right. It was literally breathtaking. It was not just that beautiful Red Lagoon, where flamingos join the llamas. There is also the Green Lagoon – a milky, viscous jade so rich in lead and arsenic that no sensible creature would approach.

That evening, we checked into the Luna Salada, a hotel sculpted entirely of salt, overlooking the world's largest and highest salt lake: the Salar de Uyuni. It stretches flat over 12,000 square kilometres and is snow-blindingly white.

Unit 22

1 20

Speaker 1: Well, the weather's certainly changed a lot since I was a boy. We used to have much colder winters then – I can remember skating on the river here and it never freezes over enough to do that now – so in some ways I can relate to what they say about global warming. But actually I think the papers make far too much of it. There are always changes and fluctuations in temperature. I remember my granddad saying that summers were much warmer when he was young. So I think it's just that things go round in cycles and I don't think we need to be all that concerned about reducing our carbon footprint and all that sort of thing.

Speaker 2: My parents go on at great length about the implications of climate change and what individuals should be doing to minimise its impact. But in fact I don't think that the average person in the street can do all that much on his or her own. Governments need to work together if we're going to see any substantial improvements and they're just not cooperating as much as they should. It's really very short-sighted, because I just don't believe it's possible to exaggerate the risks that climate change will involve. It may seem stupid to some people, but it's an issue that actually sometimes keeps me awake at night.

Speaker 3: I did a research project at college into climate change and found it very interesting – my prime objective was to see how it's affecting different countries and what various international organisations are doing to try to improve the situation. What struck me was the fact that we talk a lot about global warming. But in fact the result might be that some countries actually get colder. For example, it seems that the North Atlantic Drift, the current that keeps the waters round Britain relatively warm may change direction and start flowing from the Arctic to the Caribbean rather than the other way round.

Speaker 4: No one can argue with the fact that that the weather is changing. Some people try to say that it's all being exaggerated but that's clearly not the case. Haven't you seen all that stuff about the melting of the polar ice caps? I wonder if there'll be any ice left there by the time my kids are grown up. I just wonder, though, whether it might in fact be quite nice for some people. We normally have cold winters and not very warm summers. I'd be quite happy if we had hot summers and if I didn't have to spend so much on heating in the winter.

Speaker 5: Some people try to say that it's governments and international organisations that need to act to have any positive impact on the problem of climate change. But I think that's a bit defeatist. We shouldn't just sit back and imagine that it's up to other people – we each have to really take the situation on board and do everything we possibly can. I walk or ride my bike everywhere and if I do need to go far, then I take a bus or train. I've no intention of ever buying a car – it's a selfish thing to think only about what's of advantage to you personally, rather than considering future generations and the world they're going to inherit.

Unit 24

1 21

The phenomenon of citizen journalism is quite a recent one, but one that I'm sure you're all familiar with. I'll attempt to give a brief overview here of what it is, and how it came about. Essentially, it's where you get members of the public playing an active role in the process of collecting, analysing, reporting and disseminating news and information. This is quite different from 'traditional' methods of professional journalism. One of the basic ideas behind citizen journalism is that ordinary people, people with no professional training in journalism, can use the tools of modern technology and the Internet to create, change or fact-check media on their own or in collaboration with others. For instance, you might write about a city council meeting on, let's say, your blog. Or you could 'argue' with a newspaper feature in its comment section, or on a social networking site. Or you might take a photo or video of something happening right in front of you and put it online within seconds. I often get asked what I think about this. Is serious journalism being pushed aside? Are professional journalists, photographers, reporters going to lose their jobs?

Well, to put it simply, no. Of course, these concerns are valid, but when people want news, real news, and to find out what's really happening in the world, they almost always seek out one or two trusted sources. And what's happening more and more is that trusted, professional news providers are collecting the huge mass of public-generated photos, videos and opinions, editing them, and displaying them alongside proper journalistic items. Public contributions are becoming a valuable, and sometimes very insightful complement to standard news coverage. And in fact, most examples of citizen journalism that you read aren't on some private blog, or social-networking site – you read them on a trusted news website, already edited, proofread, and checked by professional journalists.

Answer key

Unit 1

Reading

1 1 D 2 F 3 G 4 C 5 A 6 E

Vocabulary

1 1 B 2 D 3 A 4 C 5 C 6 B 7 A 8 D

Conditionals

1 1 g 2 b 3 j 4 e 5 d 6 a 7 i 8 f
  9 c 10 h

2 1 It would be better ~~whether~~ **if** we could meet
   more often.
  2 We would like to know **if** ~~whether~~ or not you
   will be ready on the wedding day.
  3 I **would** also ~~would~~ like to say that the bus was
   late.
  4 It **would** ~~should~~ be advisable to arrive earlier
   next time.
  5 It might **even** be ~~even~~ possible to borrow the
   books from him.
  6 If it will ~~to~~ make you feel better, I will close the
   window.

3 **Suggested answers**
  1 If you require any further information, please
   don't hesitate to contact me.
  2 If you turn to page ten of the report, you'll find
   a summary.
  3 Were it not for Alison, the company would
   be in trouble now. / If it wasn't for Alison, the
   company would be in trouble now.
  4 Open the window, if it makes you feel cooler.
  5 I'll see Jane tonight, unless she's busy.

Unit 2

Writing

1 **Suggested answers**
  1 great / lovely
  2 really
  3 buy
  4 like you planned / as you planned
  5 I think
  6 I'm attaching / I'm sending
  7 am back at work / have gone back to work
  8 I don't get back
  9 'd love to hear from you again
  10 hope I hear from you soon / 'm looking forward
   to hearing from you soon

Listening

1 1 A 2 C
2 1 B 2 A
3 1 B 2 A
4 1 d 2 b 3 g 4 a 5 c 6 f 7 e

Dependent prepositions

1 1 with 2 for 3 for 4 on 5 with 6 for
  7 from 8 into 9 to 10 to 11 on 12 to
  13 to 14 on 15 in
2 1 On 2 to 3 for 4 in 5 in / over 6 on
3 1 I am writing to inform you about some problems
   with your service.
  2 There are many people who take part in
   sports.
  3 We stayed in the hotel **for** five days.
  4 Apart from that, we had to pay **for** breakfast,
   lunch and other costs.
  5 They have a good variety of food as well **as** good
   quality.
  6 Therefore, I would like to ask for a refund **from**
   your company.
  7 I would like to draw your attention **to** the areas
   which need to be improved.
  8 The reason **for** this meeting is to collect money
   for poor children.

Unit 3

Listening

1 1 isolation
  2 rural / non-urban communities
  3 photographers
  4 personal assistants
  5 creativity
  6 sports people
  7 behaviour / behavior
  8 exposure
2 1 b 2 d 3 i 4 a 5 h 6 j 7 c 8 e
  9 g 10 f
3 1 in the public interest
  2 made public
  3 claim to fame
  4 overnight fame
  5 fame and fortune
  6 constant exposure
  7 seek publicity
  8 private life
  9 the rich and famous
  10 celebrity status

Wishes and regrets

  1 people realised what it's like to be famous
  2 not to have to do so many TV interviews
  3 it wasn't such a busy day
  4 I'd studied to be a doctor
  5 I retrained so that I can / could do a different job
  6 film directors supported / would support their actors more
  7 my kids find a less stressful job
  8 I had more fans in the USA
  9 I had moved to a smaller town last year
  10 be recognised in the street than not be known at all

Reading and Use of English

1 1 A 2 A 3 D 4 B 5 C 6 D 7 A 8 C
2 1 them 2 that 3 as 4 When 5 being
  6 up 7 into 8 why

Unit 4

Reading and Use of English

1 1 A 2 C 3 B 4 D 5 B 6 C 7 A 8 C

Listening

1 1 location
  2 social programme officers
  3 unit guide
  4 research paper
  5 cost of living
  6 employment
  7 gender balance
  8 accommodation

Vocabulary

1 1 a short description, general information
  2 during, or for all of the night
  3 abroad
  4 cloudy
  5 on the next page
  6 eat too much
  7 a mistake made by a failure to notice something
2 1 widen
  2 straightened
  3 tighten
  4 lengthen
  5 thicken
  6 strenghen
  7 broadens
  8 whiten
3 1 leaves
  2 fish
  3 series
  4 passers-by
  5 analyses
  6 halves
  7 stimuli
  8 indexes / indices
  9 media
  10 selves

Modals and semi-modals (1)

1 1 ability 2 negative certainty 3 permission
  4 order 5 request 6 theoretical possibility
2 1 couldn't 2 Can / Could 3 can't have
  4 Can / Could 5 could / might 6 might
  7 could have 8 could / might
3 1 wasn't able to 2 do I have to 3 needed
  4 had to 5 should be able to
  6 needn't have
4 1 You **should either** buy a bike or a motorbike.
  2 ✓
  3 ✓

4 You **only have** to remember to enrol for the exam at least a month before.

5 I **always need** to keep up with the latest news.

Unit 5

Relative clauses

1 Suggested answers

1 I am writing with reference to the MBA course, which I understand starts at any time.

2 If possible, I would like to start in September, when I return from my annual holiday.

3 I would like to take the course in my home country, where I will have access to the internet and good libraries.

4 I graduated from (…) two years ago, where I studied Politics and Economics and gained a BSc Honours degree.

5 I am currently employed by the plastics company Wisbro, where I work in the Sales and Marketing department.

6 You can obtain a reference from Sven Larsson, the Marketing manager with whom I have worked closely for two years.

2 Suggested answers

1 There were about 15 students who **were** selected to participate in this programme.

2 I couldn't meet my friend Ann, who **lives** in St Andrews.

3 I hope that everyone who **wants** to take the test will pass it.

4 The opening hours are 8 am to 10 pm, **which** is perfect for all the students.

5 More ingredients from different seasons are used together, **which** provides more variety.

6 I do not know where **you** found the information.

7 You can also go to the Tourist Board to see **which** are the places to visit.

8 I would be very pleased if I could receive a written notification about what the company **is** going to do.

9 Many people can't imagine what **life would** be like without their car.

10 Don't you remember what Denise's wedding **was** like?

11 The book explains to us **what** the challenges **are** for the next century.

12 Of course, there are still women **who** stop working at the time they marry.

Listening

1 Part 1
   1 H   2 F   3 A   4 G   5 B
   Part 2
   1 G   2 E   3 B   4 H   5 D

Reading

1 1 B   2 C   3 D   4 A   5 A   6 A   7 D   8 D
   9 B   10 C

Unit 6

Listening

1 1 despair   2 IL B L8   3 160   4 4.1 trillion
   5 1993   6 doctors   7 embarrassing
   8 university students   9 evolve
   10 in my opinion   11 LOL   12 poetry

2 1 make
   2 catch
   3 catch
   4 have
   5 have
   6 make
   7 have
   8 make

3 1 made the effort
   2 made the point; have; effect / impact on
   3 having an argument
   4 made contact
   5 slow to catch on
   6 caught off guard

Phrasal verbs (1)

1 1 up   2 up   3 up; back   4 out; back
   5 on; over   6 through

2 1 look up   2 give / hand (it) in
   3 looked (it) through   4 pad (it) out
   5 give / hand (mine) in   6 saw (my sister) off
   7 stopped over   8 touching down   9 get / got in
   10 is booking / will book into
   11 is closing / will close down
   12 handing (my notice) in   13 setting up
   14 take on

Vocabulary

1 **1** do; best **2** took; photos **3** do; housework
4 made; mistake **5** make; effort
6 make; complaint **7** had; time **8** took; chance
9 do; favour **10** takes / has; nap
11 take; seriously **12** took; responsibility

2 **1** We simply want to **have** a nice time together.
2 I **had** such a good time in Chile.
3 If you **have** any problems, call me at the hotel.
4 We do not have time to **have** a full meal during the lunch break.
5 Why don't we **have** a barbecue?
6 Mobile phones have **had** a great impact on us.
7 There was no social programme at the summer school while I was there, but I **made** very good friends.
8 I think that some changes should be **made** to improve the museum.
9 With some effort, some really great improvements can be **made**.
10 I would also like to **make** a few suggestions about some different activities.
11 They are feeling unhealthy because they don't **do** enough sport.
12 He had no possibility of **doing** the exam.

3 **1** take **2** get **3** did **4** take **5** conducted
6 attract **7** go **8** had

Unit 7

Reading

1 **1** A **2** D **3** C **4** B **5** A **6** B

Reason, result and purpose

1 (**Possible answers**)
1 The business is experiencing some problems as a result of the recent rise in oil prices.
2 The company's difficulties stem from poor decisions made last year.
3 As a consequence of delays to the CEO's flight, the meeting began much later than expected.
4 Installing a new software system has resulted in some initial problems for staff.
5 I hope my absence next week won't give rise to any difficulties for the company.
6 Due to the fact that we were slow to take advantage of new technologies, we've fallen behind our competitors.
7 As Jason has a lot of experience in exports, the company was keen to recruit him.

Reading and Use of English

1 **1** C **2** A **3** A **4** B **5** A **6** B **7** C **8** C

Unit 8

Reading and Use of English

1 **1** around / round / about / across **2** far
3 another **4** for **5** that **6** on **7** last **8** of

2 **1** advances / advancements **2** revolutionary
3 deserving **4** productivity **5** historians
6 recognition **7** unexpected **8** awake / wakeful

Modals and semi-modals (2)

1 **1** used to
2 would
3 should
4 had to
5 would
6 should have
7 must have
8 should
9 had to
10 ought

2 **1** would **2** should **3** should **4** would
5 could

Reading

1 **1** D, E **2** B **3** F **4** C **5** D **6** B **7** A, F
8 C, D

2 **Suggested answers**
positive: key; successful; desirable; non-stop; no-holds-barred; innovative; quickly; efficiently; up-to-date; world-beating; unrivalled
negative: slow start; dilapidated; stalking; swarming; lurk; extravagant

Listening

1 **1** money-saving
2 developer
3 tutorial
4 timetable
5 interaction
6 social skills
7 over-attending

2 **1** P **2** P **3** P **4** P **5** N **6** N

Unit 9

Listening

1 1 A   2 C
2 1 B   2 A
3 1 B   2 A
4 1 raise
  2 give
  3 come
  4 have
  5 be
  6 bump
  7 pass
  8 take
  9 traffic
  10 gap

Future forms

1 **Suggested answers**
  going to try to rent … when they are ready … may
  be a bit cheaper
  will be built … will be in easy reach … are likely to
  be snapped up
  should place the main emphasis on what will
  happen, where it will happen and why it will
  happen
  will soon have completed … will be going on sale …
  going to have to put up with…
  will contribute to
  should do their utmost to… will have to maintain

2 1 *will* is more common; *will* is used more to make
  a confident prediction about the future; *going to* is
  used more for plans or intentions.
  2 *will; should; will have to; may*

Vocabulary

1 1 currently
  2 in easy reach of
  3 snapped up
  4 are in charge of
  5 going on sale
  6 put up with
  7 lend its backing to
  8 contribute to
  9 do their utmost to
  10 simultaneously

Reading and Use of English

1 1 D   2 B   3 B   4 D   5 A   6 C   7 B   8 D
2 (One mark for each phrase given in between each
  slash)
  2 extension / came to the conclusion
  3 the reason for / the rapid growth
  4 come round to / the idea of
  5 like as / congested/crowded as it
  6 to be / in Jack's shoes

Unit 10

Reading

1 1 D   2 B   3 B   4 C   5 B

Listening

1 1 C   2 C   3 D   4 A

Vocabulary

1 1 U-turn
  2 drizzly
  3 bubbling up
  4 straightforward
  5 dismal
  6 fostered
  7 a few years down the line
2 1 force   2 unromantic   3 desire   4 make holy
  5 enter   6 get married
  7 annoying self-satisfaction   8 understanding
  9 showing off

3

Verb	Noun	Adjective
restrain	restraint	restrained
rationalise	(ir)rationality	(ir)rational
simplify	simplicity	simple
invest	investment / investor	invested
cease	cessation	ceaseless
enslave	slavery	slavish
sacrifice	sacrifice	sacrificial
suspect	suspect / suspicion	suspicious
fail	failure	failed / failing
–	disaster	disastrous
invent	invention / inventor	invented / inventive
darken	darkness / the dark	dark
formalise	formality	formal

4 1 propose 2 invest 3 disaster 4 simplified
5 suspicious 6 disastrous 7 inventive

Participle clauses

1 Suggested answers
1 Not having planned it, I did it unromantically one drizzly Monday night outside the pub at closing time.
2 In that world, I was a witch, turning boys into frogs.
3 Our commitment having already been made, there is, in a sense, no reason to get married at all.
4 But then, beginning to think about it and to take on board his arguments, I re-examined my objections.
5 Having begun to think of marriage as a possible choice out of many possible choices, and not a destiny imposed upon me, I found that it didn't seem quite so awful after all.
6 Having got rid of the objections, I started to be able to see certain advantages.
7 Not having darkened the door of a single store's bridal department, I'm not going for white, but green.

Unit 11

Reading

1 1 C 2 D 3 G 4 F 5 A 6 E

Vocabulary

1 1 lure 2 siblings 3 promotes 4 dilute
5 install 6 browse 7 stand for
2 1 installed 2 browse 3 stands for 4 lured
5 promote

Reported speech

1 1 promised 2 warned 3 insisted 4 invited
5 offered 6 agreed / asked
7 advised / recommended 8 told
2 1 John not to let them use the Internet
2 having bought / buying
3 to take Sara's laptop away
4 leaving the laptop switched on
5 about his children playing / that his children played
6 teaching children
7 him not to stare at the screen / him against playing

Reading and Use of English

1 1 replaced 2 preferred 3 heights 4 desirable
5 remove 6 offensive / offending 7 meanwhile
8 alternative

Unit 12

-ing forms

1 1 imagine 2 resent 3 enjoy 4 waste time
5 interested in 6 can't help
7 look forward to 8 give up 9 miss
10 get used to
2 1 to have 2 taking 3 to make 4 to complete
5 turning down
3 1 This website is aimed **at** helping people find a job.
2 The course has been very useful **in** improving my business English.
3 If you are afraid **of** missing the train, arrive early at the station.
4 I am capable **of** translating all the necessary details.
5 You cancelled it **without** giving us a reasonable explanation.

4 **1** to get **2** printing **3** to spend **4** to hear
 5 to consider **6** using **7** booking **8** writing

Listening

1 Part 1
 1 G 2 E 3 C 4 F 5 H
 Part 2
 1 F 2 A 3 C 4 G 5 D

Reading

1 **1** D **2** B **3** A **4** D

Unit 13

Reading and Use of English

1 **1** which
 2 been
 3 the
 4 In
 5 but / yet / however / though
 6 to
 7 had / needed / wanted / ought
 8 if / when(ever) / where(ver)

Vocabulary

1 **1** terrified **2** exquisite **3** excruciating
 4 hilarious **5** deafening **6** famished
 7 furious **8** vibrant **9** spotless

Past tenses and the present perfect

1 **1** were floating / floated; realised; felt
 2 had lived / had been living; had had
 3 finished; started
 4 had never done; was
 5 was; had painted
 6 were; had been decorating
 7 had seen; seemed
 8 did you last hear
 9 have visited
 10 haven't been uploaded
 11 hadn't seen; bumped
 12 had been following / had followed; was going
 13 haven't had
 14 was driving; was taking / took place
 15 have been; moved
 16 Has anybody seen
 17 was reading; began
 18 lifted / was lifting; reached / were reaching
 19 had been repaired; had fallen / was falling
 20 had been living; was

2 **1** became **2** has become **3** has become
 4 has changed **5** have improved
 6 have increased **7** have been **8** has never
 9 was given **10** were

3 **1** For five years Kathy, **has been learning** English
    at a private language school.
 2 Lately, the business **has been looking** up.
 3 I know that she **has been dreaming** about
    Australia for over 10 years.
 4 This show **has been** on our screens every day of
    the week since 2000.
 5 For some years, a revolution **has been taking**
    place regarding the role women play in society.

Reading and Use of English

1 **1** has been studying
 2 had explained the colour chart did
 3 despite having redecorated / redecorating
 4 it when her art was admired
 5 subject to the college authorities agreeing
 6 has declined over the last
2 **1** remarkable
 2 concentration
 3 impolite
 4 friendships / friendliness
 5 Unfortunately
 6 inability
 7 conclusion
 8 performance

Unit 14

Vocabulary

1 **a** 3 **b** 1 **c** 4 **d** 2 **e** 6 **f** 7 **g** 5
2 **1** down **2** out **3** over **4** round **5** into
3 **1** talk into; talk out of; talk round
 2 talk over
 3 talk down

The passive

1 **1** have been adapted **2** are aimed
 3 is disadvantaged **4** has been written / is written
 5 be summarised **6** has been done
 7 be written **8** be ruined **9** be read
 10 is given

2 Suggested answers
2 will have to get / have my eyes tested
3 am going to get / have it made into a poster
4 had it redecorated
5 will have to get / have it copied
6 get / have it checked
7 will have to get/have it dry cleaned
8 get / have my hair cut

3 1 I can promise you that nobody **has been harmed** so far by a member of the medical service.
2 I **have been invited** to take part again as interpreter.
3 This new satellite TV series **has been shown** in our country for the last couple of weeks.
4 Along a path, which **has been built / was built** for visitors, you will get to a row of farmers' houses.
5 Some of the classes on your course **could have been prepared** better.
6 For example, this book **has been written / was written** with children in mind.

Listening

1 1 B 2 A 3 C 4 B 5 A 6 C

Unit 15

Reading

1 1 D 2 G 3 B 4 F 5 A 6 E

Vocabulary

1 1 c 2 e 3 a 4 b 5 d
2 1 d 2 a 3 e 4 b 5 c
3 1 d 2 c 3 a 4 e 5 b

The infinitive

1 1 failed 2 to gain; pretended
3 tend / are supposed 4 intend / want
5 managed / failed 6 want; supposed
7 arranged / were supposed 8 afford; invite

2 1 to be sitting / to sit
2 to phone / to have phoned
3 to take part / to have taken part; to sit / to be sitting / to have been sitting
4 to be covered 5 to be asked 6 not to be
7 invite 8 work 9 watch
10 To include / To have included
11 go 12 ask / to ask 13 To retire / Retiring
14 to win
15 to talk 16 to take 17 to help 18 to eat
19 to explain 20 to be

3 1 getting 2 to meet 3 interviewing
4 managing 5 getting 6 to live 7 of winning

Unit 16

Inversion

1 Suggested answers
1 In no way are we responsible for what happened.
2 Only on very rare occasions does he put in an appearance.
3 On no account should you just do what they say without thinking it through yourself.
4 No sooner had John sold his house than the one he was hoping to buy fell through.
5 Little did I imagine that I would ever meet a famous Hollywood film star.
6 At no time should you let anyone know what you are really doing here.
7 Never before have I stayed in such a bad hotel.

2 1 Not only **was the food** dull, but also the service was not what you stated in the brochure.
2 I would be pleased to try this job for one week. Only then **will I** be sure if I like it.
3 Not only **was it** wrong, but there were not enough minibuses to transport us.
4 Not only **was there** no choice for vegetarians, but also the food was inedible.
5 Some food companies believe that only in this way **can people** be interested in buying their product.
6 Perhaps **we could** do the test again?
7 Your hotel was not cheap. Nor **can I** accept that you offer high standards of service or food.
8 If I could choose any time or place, then I **would definitely** choose the US in the 1960s.
9 Anyway, you asked me what **you should** wear.
10 Not until you have passed your driving test **should you** drive a car alone.

Vocabulary

1 1 tongue 2 head 3 foot 4 heart 5 ear
6 nose 7 eye 8 hand
2 1 1a 2 1c 3 2a 4 3a 5 3c 6 5b 7 4a
8 4b 9 4c 10 8c 11 5a 12 7c 13 2b
14 7b 15 6a 16 7a 17 8a 18 8b 19 2c
20 1b 21 6c 22 3b 23 6b 24 5c

Reading and Use of English

1 1 Although 2 of 3 themselves 4 that
5 which 6 some 7 for 8 Were

Listening

1 1 A 2 B

2 1 detect 2 deliver 3 respond
4 sensors; processed 5 activating

Unit 17

Reading

2 Suggested answers

A 1 a car
  2 wheelbase; roofline; gear stick; dashboard;
    seats
  3 wasted space; creative thinking; Equal
    ingenuity; Some are better than others; what's
    the use of it?

B 1 a restaurant
  2 dining; dishes; menu; roast duckling; sweet
    pineapple and vanilla sauce
  3 mistakes; potential for disaster; strange but
    true; adequate; sickly sweet

C 1 a film
  2 movie; watchable; setting
  3 chocolate box; sweet and gooey and enjoyably
    bad; always watchable; beautiful; kind; silly;
    beautifully executed; a haven

D 1 an album or CD
  2 tracks; music; songs
  3 nothing … special; big change; one of the
    great songs

2 1 purposes 2 true 3 sweet 4 the dots
5 refuge 6 love 7 disappointed

Reading and Use of English

(One mark is given for each phrase given in
between each slash.)

1 1 is supposed / to have
2 couldn't believe / my eyes
3 may have / left her newspaper on
4 we had spent / less on
5 to come up with / a title
6 object to/mind being / the centre of

Articles

1 1 **The** information you find on **the** Internet …
2 Her boyfriend is **a** solicitor.
3 He is **the** solicitor you were reading about in **the**
  newspaper **a** week ago.
4 I earn about £8,000 **a** year from setting and
  marking exams.
5 **The** Smith family have **a** gardener who comes in
  from time to time, who they pay by **the** hour.
6 We should have dinner together at **the** Holiday
  Inn in New Square some time in **the** next few
  weeks.
7 We spent **a** week on holiday in **the** Seychelles
  but I spent most of **the** week in bed as I caught **a**
  nasty cold.
8 **The** family are all in different places this week
  – Joan has gone to **the** US and Monty is in
  India, while Sue has gone by car to **the** north
  of Scotland and Bob has taken **the** / **a** train to
  France.

2 1 talks sense
2 to be out of pocket
3 sighed with relief
4 sets sail
5 was lying face down
6 caught fire
7 by word of mouth
8 make way for

4 1 I'm afraid I only have a little money.
2 I've got a few euros.
3 Each girl in the class has her own email address.
4 Few people pass their driving test the first time.
5 He has little experience of hard manual work.

5 1 You may have to queue for **a** couple of hours.
2 I have been in London for **a** few years.
3 We have **a** plenty of different programmes on
  TV.
4 We are having an athletics competition ~~the~~ next
  month.
5 We believe that opening the centre to **the** public
  would be a good solution.
6 The speech was cancelled at **the** last minute.
7 I'm sure she will invite you to have ~~the~~ breakfast
  with her.
8 We should use ~~the~~ public transport more often
  and not depend on cars.

Unit 18

Listening

1 1 A 2 B 3 D 4 C

Emphasis

1 1 What I find hard when I meet someone new is making small talk.

2 What parents usually enjoy talking about is their children.

3 All you need to do to be thought of as a good conversationalist is to ask someone about themselves and then sit back and listen to the answer.

4 The sensible thing to do when you're making small talk is not to talk about serious topics.

5 What immediately struck me about her was her ability to make small talk.

Reading

1 1 G 2 B 3 F 4 D 5 A 6 E

Vocabulary

1 1 f 2 c 3 h 4 b 5 k 6 i 7 d 8 j
9 l 10 e 11 a 12 g

2 Suggested answers

1 it's human nature; it's second nature; it's not in his nature

2 let something go; let someone down; don't let it get you down

3 in the course of time; be on a collision course; par for the course

4 be set in your ways; set your heart on something; set the record straight

5 be in the mood for something; be in a good mood; not be in the mood to do something

Unit 19

Reading and Use of English

1 1 that 2 Everyone / Everybody 3 must
4 how 5 as 6 without 7 instead 8 few

Listening

1 1 course 2 Canada 3 well-off 4 intelligent
5 attitudes / feelings 6 average 7 (new) jacket
8 personality

2

Noun	Verb	Adverb
flattery, flatterer	flatter	flatterer
instruction, instructor	instruct	instructive
straight	straighten	straight
expectation	expect	expectant
despair	despair	desperate
application, applicant	apply	applicable, applied
compliment	compliment	complimentary

Reading and Use of English

1 1 a brief portrait of

2 go over the differences between

3 which have an influence on / over

4 to consider different ways in

5 explaining the reason for

6 point I'm trying to make

Language of persuasion

1&2 Suggested answers

1 formal, younger instructor with older learner
A: Come on. Have a go!
B: Just show me again and I'll have a go.

2 formal, manager and business consultant
A: What do you think we should do?
B: Just keep on like you are now, I guess.

3 informal, old friends
A: Could you tell me where the station is, please?
B: Certainly. I could drive you there myself on the way to the office, if you like.

4 informal, mother and child
A: What did you think of the film?
B: I'm afraid I didn't like it very much.

5 formal, sales assistant and customer
A: What on Earth do I do now?
B: Just fill in the form and then give it to the girl over there.

Unit 20

Listening

1 a 4 b 7 c 9 d 11 e 2 f 1 g 10 h 5
i 6 j 3 k 8

2 **1** how often   **2** (on) holiday(s)
3 three weeks   **4** 21% / percent
5 44% / percent   **6** 7% / percent
7 20% / percent   **8** one third
9 reputation(s) / status   **10** consumption
11 different venues

Vocabulary

1

Noun	Verb	Adjective	Adverb
difference	differ / differentiate	different	differently
finance	finance	financial	financially
system	systematise	(un)systematic	(un)systematically
respondent	respond	(un)responsive	responsively
exclusion	exclude	exclusive	exclusively
frequency	frequent	(in)frequent	(in)frequently
prevalence	prevail	prevalent	–
attribute / attribution	attribute	attributive / attributed	–
refinement	refine	(un)refined	–
superiority	–	superior	–
distinction	distinguish	(in)distinct / distinctive / distinguished	(in)distinctly

2 **1** distinct   **2** frequency   **3** prevalent
   4 attributed   **5** finance   **6** exclusive
   7 responded   **8** refining   **9** superiority
   10 difference   **11** system

Hypothesising

1 **1** hypothetical   **2** imagine   **3** assume
   4 Were   **5** assumption   **6** Allowing
   7 Provided / Providing   **8** Speculating
   9 wonder   **10** suppose
2 **1** for   **2** if   **3** whether / if   **4** to be   **5** offered
3 **Suggested answers**
   1 As long as she gets the questions she's prepared for, she should do very well in the exam.
   2 If I were you, I'd resign on the spot.
   3 He's only agreed to help finance the project on the assumption that she is also going to put in an equal amount.
   4 If we had anticipated what problems might arise, we would never have embarked on such a complex venture.
   5 I'd love to know whether Laura still thinks about me.

6 What if we make no changes at all for the time being?
7 Let's take the hypothetical case of a single mother bringing up two children.
8 If only I knew how she felt about things.
9 I wonder if they will win the World Cup.
10 Suppose I ask her out on a date and she says 'no'?

Unit 21

Listening

2 **a** 2   **b** 1   **c** 2   **d** 3   **e** 2   **f** 1   **g** 1   **h** 1
   i 3   **j** 3   **k** 3   **l** 2   **m** 1   **n** 3   **o** 3
3 **a** 3   **b** 2   **c** 1   **d** 1   **e** 2   **f** 3   **g** 1

Range of grammatical structures

1 Jordan Romero, a 13-year-old American, <u>has</u> his sights on one of the Wonders of the World, not for his geography homework, but for his own very real goal – <u>climbing</u> it. He <u>wants to reach</u> the summit of Mount Everest, in an attempt <u>to become</u> the youngest person who <u>has conquered</u> the mountain. Jordan, along with his parents, <u>will attempt</u> the climb. Mt. Everest <u>is</u> part of Jordans's ambition <u>to bag</u> the tallest peaks on each of the seven continents. He <u>told</u> his dad about what he <u>would like to do</u>. His dad <u>didn't try to talk</u> him out of it. He just <u>explained</u> the difficulties and what he <u>would have to do</u>, and they <u>started training</u> right away.

2 **1** combines   **2** was inspired   **3** seeing
   4 started   **5** to climb   **6** added
   7 expressing/who express   **8** to be faced
   9 have been known   **10** result
3 **1** does   **2** but   **3** as   **4** if   **5** had   **6** there
   7 why   **8** a   **9** before / so   **10** will   **11** without
   12 which   **13** has   **14** it   **15** from

Vocabulary

1 **Suggested answers**
famous; spectacular; luxury; delicious; varied; first-class; spacious; well-designed; amazing; comfort; frequent; many fascinating; no additional costs; rest assured; extremely cheap; holiday of a lifetime; you have always dreamed of
2 **1** f   **2** a   **3** g   **4** b   **5** e   **6** h   **7** d   **8** c
3 **Suggested answers**
   1 because
   2 accommodation
   3 if you had seen
   4 Speaking of

5 looking forward to getting
6 led to
7 we had been promised that we would visit
8 turned out
9 had to
10 I hope

Unit 22

Listening

1 1 h 2 e 3 a 4 c 5 f

2

Noun	Verb	Adjective
fluctuation	fluctuate	fluctuating
cycle	cycle	cyclical
reduction	reduce	reduced
implication	imply	implied
minimum	minimise	minimal
cooperation	cooperate	cooperative
improvement	improve	improved / improving
significance	signify	significant
exaggeration	exaggerate	exaggerated
intention	intend	intended
consideration	consider	considered
inheritance	inherit	inherited

Vocabulary

1 1 cumulative 2 torrential 3 heat 4 below
  5 commitment 6 footprint 7 melting
  8 Drought
2 1 fluctuate 2 minimise 3 exaggerated
  4 reduce 5 inherit 6 co-operation
  7 significant 8 intention 9 consideration
  10 improvement

Interpreting and comparing

1 whereas, on the other hand, while, in contrast, however, although
2 1 rapid 2 marked 3 steep 4 falls and rises
  5 steady
3 **Sample answer**
The line graph shows changes in average global temperatures between 1880 and 2010. From the years 1880 to around 1890, there was no significant rise in temperatures. However, in the following decade, there was a slight increase, with temperatures rising around two degrees. From then, while there was some fluctuation in temperatures, there was a small, gradual rise until 1970. At that time, temperatures had risen approximately four degrees on the 1880 average. After this date, there was a significant change in the pattern. Moreover, a sharp, sudden increase could be seen, with temperatures rising around one degree every ten years. This steep rise in temperatures has continued until the present day. In addition, it can be said that since the 1970s, there has been no significant drop in temperatures.

To sum up, it can be seen that there was no significant change in global temperatures until the 1970s, after which, there began a marked rise which shows no sign of changing.

4 1 You will find public telephones both in the airport and in the station ~~but~~ and also in the streets.
  2 There was no special service ~~or~~ and the food was not especially great.
  3 We can stay at home without seeing anybody ~~and~~ or speaking to a 'real' person for ages.
  4 If someone does not feel good mentally **or** feels lonely, he will not work well.
  5 I hope you will find the programme very lively **and** sociable.
  6 I'd like to find work in an insurance company ~~and~~ or a bank.

5 1 Even **though** he doesn't like the course, he is studying because he has to.
  2 On the first evening, they organised a guided tour for the tourists ~~therefore~~ so (that) it would be a good introduction to the city for them.
  3 ~~However~~ Although / **Even though** the itinerary was well planned, everything was ruined by that coach, which stopped working on Wednesday.
  4 ~~During~~ While travelling from the airport to the train station, I lost my baggage.
  5 Day two was supposed to be at a typical English restaurant, ~~while~~ whereas it was really at a hamburger restaurant.
  6 You will be provided with exercise books. ~~Although,~~ **However**, sometimes you will need to buy extra ones.

Reading and Use of English

1 **1** inhabitants **2** psychologically **3** hardships
  4 relaxed **5** desperately **6** personality
  7 disproportionate **8** influential

2 **1** there is little / no likelihood of
  2 to take many factors into account / to take
    account of many factors
  3 a significant increase in the
  4 temperatures rose sharply
  5 making a significant reduction in

Unit 23

Reading

1 **1** no **2** Having **3** as **4** but **5** be
  6 without **7** Although / While **8** to

Vocabulary

1 **1** d **2** g **3** e **4** i **5** j **6** h **7** b **8** f
  9 a **10** c

2 **1** regret **2** kind **3** choice **4** prompt
  5 appreciate **6** grateful **7** response / reply
  8 hesitate **9** of / dated **10** hope

Phrasal verbs (2)

1 **1** A **2** C **3** C **4** C **5** B **6** C **7** A
  8 B **9** B **10** C

2 **a** get across **b** fall through **c** turn up
  d put (something) down to (something else)
  e single out **f** put off **g** write off
  h get on with **i** break out **j** bring out

3 **1** I phoned a taxi company to ~~know~~ **find out** the
    average rate from the airport to the station.
  2 The problems started from the same moment I
    ~~went into~~ **got on** the coach.
  3 You take the number one bus and you ~~go down~~
    get off at the 11th stop.
  4 You might be able to **take part ~~at~~ in** our next
    event next July.
  5 The construction of the new blocks of flats could
    be **paid for** by the grant the city has got.
  6 You should organise parties for everyone to **get
    to know** his or her colleagues.
  7 A new, good bus is indispensable if we **go ~~to~~ on** a
    day trip to Stratford-upon-Avon.

4 **1** find out **2** get on **3** get off **4** get off
  5 get to know **6** learn

Unit 24

Use of English

1 **1** at **2** up **3** itself **4** later **5** its **6** with
  7 there **8** no / few

Listening

1 **1** analysing **2** modern technology
  3 (city) council **4** serious **5** sources
  6 providers **7** insightful **8** edited

Vocabulary

1 **1** bulletin **2** non-biased **3** feature
  4 coverage **5** insightful **6** reporter
  7 journalist **8** complement

2 **1** give an overview
  2 collect / give / find out information
  3 take / play a video
  4 put something online
  5 lose a job
  6 find out what's happening
  7 play an active role

3 **1** attend **2** achieve **3** conducted **4** meets
  5 draw **6** take

Reading and Use of English

1 **1** innovative **2** breadth **3** rigorous
  4 expertise **5** stress-free **6** comparably
  7 contents **8** requirements

Connecting words

1 **1** as well as **2** In spite of **3** though **4** but
  5 However, **6** As **7** Owing to **8** such
  9 so fast that **10** Thanks to **11** in case
  12 No matter **13** as **14** anyway **15** However

Unit 25

Reading

1 **1** C **2** D **3** A **4** D

2 **a** identical twins **b** genes **c** privileged
  d incoherent **e** pursuits

3 **1** appropriate **2** definitely **3** beginning
  4 ✓ **5** ✓ **6** accommodation **7** ✓
  8 successful **9** career **10** ✓ **11** ✓
  12 healthy **13** disappointed **14** ✓

Complex sentences and adverbials

1 1 He'll show the new office junior ~~how~~ **what** to do.
  2 ✓
  3 ✓
  4 This is the marketing manager, ~~who's~~ **whose** office is just down the corridor.
  5 ~~Who~~ **What** I can't stand are people ~~which~~ **who** complain about everything.
  6 I think I've found a time **when** ~~where~~ we can both meet.
  7 ✓
  8 ✓
  9 ✓
 10 That's the man who ~~he~~ will appear in court tomorrow.

2 1 d   2 f   3 a   4 c   5 e   6 b

3 1 Advertising is an industry which / that wields considerable power within Western societies.
  2 This article is by Kathy Myers, who is the editor of one of the top women's magazines.
  3 The final chapter of the book, which deals with the change in attitudes to opera, will be expanded.
  4 That's Mr Williams who I was talking to just yesterday. / That's Mr Williams to whom I was just talking yesterday.
  5 Some people, a few of whom live in the villages in the foothills, still speak the local dialect.
  6 Our research into language has produced some interesting results which show that as many new words are coming into the language as old ones that are dying out.
  7 We listened to recordings of several dialects, many of which I'd never heard before.
  8 There were two fantastic photos for the book, one of which was chosen as the front cover.

4 1 One member has also complained about your booking system, ~~that~~ **which** should be improved urgently.
  2 The aim of this report is to suggest a magazine for students who ~~they~~ would like to study Greek.
  3 I want to give you information about my neighbour, ~~which~~ **who** I have known for a long time.
  4 The opening hours are from eight o'clock, ~~what~~ **which** are perfect.
  5 The exchange students, ~~that~~ **who** will be visiting you from July, do not require special food.

Use of English

1 1 wished she had paid more
  2 was no justification for such
  3 to think whenever I take
  4 even if / though he's
  5 despite the fact that she practised / despite her practising

Acknowledgements

The authors and publishers acknowledge the following sources of copyright material and are grateful for the permissions granted. While every effort has been made, it has not always been possible to identify the sources of all the material used, or to trace all copyright holders. If any omissions are brought to our notice, we will be happy to include the appropriate acknowledgements on reprinting.

The publisher has used its best endeavours to ensure that the URLs for external websites referred to in this book are correct and active at the time of going to press. However, the publisher has no responsibility for the websites and can make no guarantee that a site will remain live or that the content is or will remain appropriate.

Development of this publication has made use of the Cambridge English Corpus (CEC). The CEC is a computer database of contemporary spoken and written English, which currently stands at over one billion words. It includes British English, American English and other varieties of English. It also includes the Cambridge Learner Corpus, developed in collaboration with the Cambridge English Language Assessment. Cambridge University Press has built up the CEC to provide evidence about language use that helps to produce better language teaching materials.

This product is informed by the English Vocabulary Profile, built as part of English Profile, a collaborative programme designed to enhance the learning, teaching and assessment of English worldwide. Its main funding partners are Cambridge University Press and Cambridge English Language Assessment and its aim is to create a 'profile' for English linked to the Common European Framework of Reference for Languages (CEF). English Profile outcomes, such as the English Vocabulary Profile, will provide detailed information about the language that learners can be expected to demonstrate at each CEF level, offering a clear benchmark for learners' proficiency. For more information, please visit www.englishprofile.org.

Texts

Gill Todd for the text on pp. 4–5 adapted from 'A Great Place to Go Batty' by Gill Todd, *The Times Weekend*, 29.08.98. Copyright © Gill Todd 1998; Haymarket Group for the text on p. 13 adapted from 'Stop, look, listen. Before you Buy', *What Hi Fi?*, January 1999. Reprinted with permission; Telegraph Media Group Limited for the text and listening exercise on p. 19 adapted from 'Virtually flirting with love's new language' by David Cohen, *The Telegraph*, 01.02.00, p. 30 adapted from 'Hard drive: Making a Speech' by Peter Cochrane, *The Telegraph*, 04.01.01, p. 52 (A) adapted from 'Motoring' by Neil Lyndon, *The Sunday Telegraph*, 18.06.00, p. 52 (B) adapted from 'Restaurants' by Matthew Norman, *The Sunday Telegraph*, 18.06.00. Copyright © Telegraph Media Group Limited 2000, 2001; Guardian News & Media Ltd for the text on p. 22 adapted from 'Zoo Management' by Nigel Nicholson, *The Guardian*, 10.02.01, p. 31 adapted from 'Will you marry me?' by Charlotte Higgins, *The Guardian*, 29.02.00. Copyright © Guardian News & Media Ltd 2000, 2001; SourceMedia Inc for the text on p. 24 adapted from 'Business Process Improvement using Cause-and-Effect Analysis and Design of Experiments' by Nari Kanna, *InfoManagement Direct*, July 2005. Reprinted with permission; Linda Sweeney for the text and listening exercise on p. 27 adapted from 'Guidelines for being a good online student' by Linda Sweeny www.learningassistance.com/2005/august/onlineguidelines. htm. Copyright © Linda Sweeny. Reproduced by permission; NI Syndication for the text on p. 34 adapted from 'Fighting the computer invasion', *The Times*, 03.01.00, p. 36 adapted from 'A shape of fins to come' by Max Glaskin, *Sunday Times Style Magazine*, 06.02.00. Copyright © NI Syndication; The Royal Institution for the text and listening exercise on p. 45 adapted from *Staying Alive: The Body in Balance. Lecture 1 – Sense and Sensitivity* by Professor Nancy Rothwell, 08.12.98. Copyright © The Royal Institution 1998. Reprinted with permission; The Independent for the text on pp. 46-47 adapted from 'Clarity in a Cold Climate' by Roger Dobson, *The Independent*, 23.12.99. Copyright © The Independent 1999; Extract on p. 52 (C) adapted from 'Preview: A guide to the week's television and radio. "A Walk in the Clouds (1995)"' by Andy Medhurst, *The Sunday Telegraph Magazine*, 18.06.00. Copyright © Telegraph Media Group Limited; Extract on p. 53 (D) adapted from a review of 'Don Henley album – Inside Job, *Country Music International*, July 2000; Cosmopolitan for the text on p. 58 adapted from 'How to sweet talk anyone' by Celeste Perron, *Cosmopolitan*, June 2000. Copyright © National Magazine Company. Reprinted with permission; Cambridge University Press for the text and listening exercise on p. 61 adapted from *Eating Out: Social Differentiation, Consumption and Pleasure*. Copyright © Alan Warde and Lydia Martens, 2000, published by Cambridge University Press. Reproduced with permission; Digital Journal Inc for the text on p. 65 adapted from 'Mount Everest ascent planned by 13 year old', www.digitaljournal.com/article/290148. Published with permission of Digital Journal.com; World Association of Newspapers, France for the text on p. 73 adapted from 'Twitter first off the mark with Hudson plane crash coverage' by Helena Deards, http://www.editorsweblog. org/multimedia/2009/01/twitter_first_off_the_mark_with hudson_p.php. Reprinted with permission; Elijah Wolfson for the text on p. 76 adapted from 'Intelligence and Genetics: Do Some People Inherit and Edge?' by Elijah Wolfson, *Motherboard (Vice)*, http:// motherboard.vice.com/blog/intelligence-and-genetics-do-some-people-inherit-an-edge. Copyright © Elijah Wolfson. Reprinted with permission.

Photos

p. 4: Paul Armiger/The Times/NewsSyndication.com; p. 5: © CraigRJD/iStockphoto; p. 7: © Catchlight Visual Services/Alamy; p. 8: Goodluz/Shutterstock; p. 10: Rex Features/Buzz Foto; p. 12: Rex Features/Startraks Photo; p. 13: © Vladislav Kochelaevskiy/ Alamy; p. 14 (T): Kristian Cabanis/age fotostock/SuperStock; p. 14 (C): YURALAITS ALBERT/Shutterstock; p. 14 (B): aastock/ Shutterstock; p. 16: Todd Warnock/Photodisc/Thinkstock; p. 18: mangostock/Shutterstock; p. 19: © Imran Ahmed/Alamy; p. 20: Anton Gvozdikov/Shutterstock; p. 20: Stockbyte/Thinkstock Images; p. 22: Published by Texere Publishing Ltd, © 2000, Nigel Nicholson. Cover illustration used with permission of David Holmes.; p. 24: © qaphotos.com/Alamy; p. 25: Reshavskyi/Shutterstock; p. 26: Jeff Greenberg/age fotostock/SuperStock; p. 29 (TL): StockLite/ Shutterstock; p. 29 (TC): YURALAITS ALBERT/Shutterstock; p. 29 (TR): Twin Design/Shutterstock; p. 29 (CL): © Radius Images/ Alamy; p. 29 (CR): Goodluz/Shutterstock; p. 29 (B): R. Gino Santa Maria/Shutterstock; p. 36: Rex Features; p. 37: © Pegaz/Alamy; p. 40: kuznetcov_konstantin/Shutterstock; p. 43 (T): asiseeit/iStockphoto; p. 43 (B): Yuri/iStockphoto; p. 44: mbbirdy/iStockphoto; p. 45: age fotostock/SuperStock; p. 46: © leemarch/fotolia; p. 51: Peter Bernik/ Shutterstock; p. 52 (T): © Ramon Grosso dolarea/Thinkstock; p. 52 (BL): © Marin Tomas/Alamy; p. 52 (BR): © Ron Chapple studios/ Hemera/Thinkstock; p. 53: © Friday/Thinkstock; p. 55: Ball at the Moulin de la Galette, 1876 (oil on canvas), Renoir, Pierre Auguste (1841-1919)/Musee d'Orsay, Paris, France/Giraudon/The Bridgeman Art Library; p. 59: ARENA Creative/Shutterstock; p. 61 (T): Digital Vision/Thinkstock; p. 61 (B): Blend_Images/iStockphoto; p. 63: asife/ Shutterstock; p. 64 (T): Stanislav Fosenbauer/Shutterstock; p. 64 (C): creighton359/iStockphoto; p. 64 (B/G): © Horizons WWP/Alamy; p. 65: Ignacio Salaverria/Shutterstock; p. 66: Zalka/Shutterstock; p. 68: NASA/Goddard Space Flight Center; p. 69: © Alexander Kaplun/ Thinkstock; p. 70: Rex Features; p. 73: Rex Features/Sipa Press; p. 74: Rex Features/Jonathan Hordle/Ray Tang; p. 76 (T): © Peter Banos/ Alamy; p. 76 (C): © CJG - Technology/Alamy; p. 76 (B): © PCN Photography/Alamy; p. 77: Olesya Feketa/Shutterstock.

Picture research by the Bill Smith Group, Inc

Recordings by Leon Chambers at The Soundhouse Ltd Recording Studios